Praise for

The Heart of Sacred Listening

"In this book, Amba Gale describes her own arduous journey towards learning '*The Heart of Sacred Listening*.' Thereby, she proves two points: 1- That Biography is a most convincing tool for teaching. 2 - That listening with the heart is indeed a sacred art worth acquiring

— **David Steindl-Rast**, Benedictine monk, author.
https://www.bibliothek-david-steindl-rast.ch/

"I absolutely love Amba and her work. If you are smart, you'll become a student of Amba's brilliant work, first by reading her wonderful, rich book, which is filled with both inspiring stories and powerful and practical advice and strategies for having your relationships work. If you do, you'll end up being a much better person, a happier person, and you'll be in touch with your own divinity as well as the divinity of others. Because Amba, herself, is a divine gift you can give yourself, I also encourage you to explore personally working with her. I promise you'll be glad you did."

— **Jack Canfield**, coauthor of the #1 *New York Times* bestselling
Chicken Soup for the Soul® series and *The Success Principles*™:
How to Get from Where You Are to Where You Want to Be

"*Mo scéal féin—scéal gach duine—My own story is everyone's story*" is an ancient Irish proverb. This age-old adage rings true between the covers of this soulful, heartwarming book.

Amba shares her own, her friends', and clients' personal stories, knowing that they are universal and will open both the minds and the hearts of every reader.

The stories and accompanying teachings are rich openings into the wholesome practice of profound listening first named by St. Benedict in the 6th century. "*Ausculta—listen with the ear of the heart*" is the very first precept of his monastic Rule.

This book is truly a precious manual for such a ritual.

May this volume for living from and attending to the sacred in our lives spread out into a world that needs its wisdom."

— **Rev. Nóirín Ní Riain**, PhD, spiritual singer, author,
theologian, and interfaith minister

"My first experience illuminated my true career aspirations and provided clarity and confidence to take bold and uncharted steps. The second time I departed the course with a greater understanding and appreciation for team, and a commitment to honor a long and important relationship. I found I could reframe this story and find the gold in words and actions that previously left me angry and confused.

My third learning was coming to peace with my legacy, and the acknowledgment that I don't have the right, or responsibility, to dictate the future. It simply isn't needed, or up to me.

Prior to reading *The Heart of Sacred Listening*, I thought the only way to have experiences like mine was through the in-person experience. Now I know that there is power in these pages, and one can immerse themselves in the discovery, learning, and practices that will give wings to those seeking amazing breakthroughs.

I recommend this book for more than a single read, but to be used as a reference manual for continued discovery and reinforcement. Happy journeys, fellow readers!"

— **David Duro**, President & CEO, Treasure Valley Family YMCA

"I've taken the Heart of Leadership course three times and have invited nearly 60 members of our organization to experience it because of the profound impact it has had on how we show up for one another as leaders and as people.

Reading *The Heart of Sacred Listening* brought the work to life in a completely new way for me. I could feel Amba telling the stories as I read, and the experience deepened the lessons even further. Listening and reading are two different experiences — and together they are incredibly powerful.

This book is not just about becoming a better leader. It's about becoming a more authentic human being and strengthening the relationships that matter most."

— **Kim Hunter,** CEO, Plymouth, Inc.

"*The Heart of Sacred Listening* carries the voice of one of the most authentic and enlightened teachers I have known—a voice that listens as deeply as it speaks. This book opens the doorway to communion and reminds us that listening is not an act of the ear, but of the heart. Amba has been both a dear friend and a guide, and her invitation to Sacred Listening reveals the divine beneath all conversation. I am grateful for her presence in my life and for the light this work brings into the world."

— **Michael Meyer**, MD, MBA, FACS, Chairman of the Board,
Pulse Heart Institute

"Amba is my "poster child" for someone who learns from her own reflection, the one attribute common to all leaders that Warren Bennis discovered and reported on in his famous book, *On Becoming a Leader*. Successful leaders learn, uniquely, from their own experiences. In her book, Amba has revealed the process she has discovered and uses for reflection. This combination of a willingness to reflect and a proven process, if used, is life-changing and transformational. I highly recommend this book!"

— Greg Merten, Vice President, Printing Supplies, HP (retired)

"I absolutely love your book! It has reinvigorated the "deep work" I began with you during *The Heart of Leadership*. This book offers timeless principles that enlighten, enliven, and truly have the power to transform lives. The stories you share are powerful and bring the content to life, while the "stopping off" points are thoughtfully placed to encourage the reader to reflect and apply the lessons. This is the book I always hoped you would write—and here it is!"

— Bill Weymer, former CEO, Town & Country Markets

"This is not a book you simply read—you engage with it. It invites deep reflection and real inner work, and the results are transformative. Even without prior experience with Amba's work, I found it profoundly impactful and will return to it again and again.

It challenges you to examine the paradigms shaping your life and, through practice, helps shift listening from something you do into a way of being. This is not a book to rush through, but one to live with—returning to it over time as your awareness deepens."

— Tim Tackett, Director of Operations, PCC Community Markets

"Even without prior experience with Amba's work, I found this book offers both immediate, life-changing shifts in thinking and a pathway for deeper, long-term self-discovery… What makes it especially compelling is how much of yourself you bring to the pages—we feel like we come to know you and want to know more by the end."

— Melissa A. Meyer, MD, Family Medicine Physician,
Novel Healthcare

"Although I had not previously worked with Amba, it has been an incredible honor to be part of this noble book and its mission. More than ever, this noisy, conflict-filled world is in deep need of the wise messages offered here—and of the kind of genuine listening this work so powerfully invites and nurtures."

— Mi Ae Lipe, Editor

"At times in my life, I've encountered books that introduce me to a fellow pilgrim—someone whose perspectives and wisdom expand my world in ways I could not have imagined. This book does exactly that.

Amba immerses the reader not in "one helpful idea," but in an entire landscape of possibility. Her unmistakable voice is here—clear, simple, playful, profound—rooted in a language that points to the otherworldly work she invites us into.

Most meaningful of all are her stories, woven seamlessly into teachings that open the heart and illuminate a path. Beautiful book, Amba. I'm so glad it will soon be in the world."

— **Ryan Joy**, Christian minister

"This insightful, content-rich book could not be more timely. If only—oh, if only!—we all had the skillset, and the courage, to really listen from and for the sacred space within each of us, this world would be a very different place.

Hooray for you, Amba, for presenting such time-tested, potentially life-altering learnings and distinctions, and for doing so in your own inimitable style. This food for thought is clearly served straight from the heart.

In addition to your soul-satiating 'main course' material, you offer the reader well-chosen side dishes: personal stories, historical perspectives, *Your Turn* prompts—all with delightful sprinkles of Amba-isms throughout. These rich ingredients combine to make this beautiful book a deeply nourishing transformational experience. Brava!"

— **Nancy Hopps**, author of *All the Courage Love Takes:
Moving through Crisis and Uncertainty with Grace, Grit,
and Gratitude* and the *Relax into Healing* audio series

"I recommend this book to anyone seeking to live a fulfilling life. Throughout *The Heart of Sacred Listening*, Amba's radiant spirit and hard-won wisdom touched, moved, and inspired me. Her writing is both clear and poetic, and reading her book is like sitting down with your best friend for a conversation that—like Amba herself—is as heartwarming and fun as it is difference-making."

— **Sanford (Sandy) Robbins**, Theatre Director,
Designer and Leader of transformational programs

the HEART of SACRED LISTENING

Also by Amba Gale

Crossing Thresholds: Island Reflections

the HEART *of* SACRED LISTENING

Transform Your
Relationships,
Your Work,
and Your Life

AMBA GALE

Published by Listening Heart Press

ISBN (paperback): 978-1-7346941-0-9
ISBN (ebook): 978-1-7346941-3-0

Book design and production by www.AuthorSuccess.com

Printed in the United States of America

Some of the materials in this book are based on material developed by Werner Erhard, and are used with permission

I dedicate this book
to two people,
for whom I am eternally grateful:

To my father, Uma,
whose vital energy,
dedication, love, and commitment
to my leading a happy, purposeful, meaningful life,
shaped my life and the lives of many others.

To my husband, Don,
whose graciousness, generosity,
extraordinary partnership, love, and profound support
have propelled all my work in the world
and created the space for this book to come into being.

Contents

Blessings for You, the Reader — xxvii
Welcome to the Heart of Sacred Listening — xxix
Introduction — 1

Part I: Awakening Your Sacred Listening for Others — 9

CHAPTER 1
Who Am I?: The Question that Opened My Life — 11

CHAPTER 2
My Dad and I: From Resistance to Love — 16

CHAPTER 3
Transforming My Relationship With My Father:
The Gift of Heart Listening — 20

CHAPTER 4
Making this Your Own: Setting Yourself up for a Breakthrough — 26

CHAPTER 5
"Files": The Stories We Tell Ourselves — 29

CHAPTER 6
Shifting Your Listening: From Asleep to Awake — 43

CHAPTER 7
A Parenting Story: From Expectation to Appreciation — 54

CHAPTER 8
"Honey, You are Just Like Me!": From Adversary to Soul Sister — 62

CHAPTER 9
It Was All in the Stopping: Awakening Awareness — 67

CHAPTER 10

What Do I Do with My Triggered Reactions?   69
Catch, Release, and Shift

CHAPTER 11

Building Relationships: The Foundation for Everything   74

CHAPTER 12

Listening Heals: Creating a Safe Space   81

CHAPTER 13

Being a Great Leader: Courage, Humility, Commitment   88

Part II: Awakening Your Sacred Listening for Yourself   95

CHAPTER 14

Integrity: Creating Wholeness and Completion   97

CHAPTER 15

Deepening Integrity in Your Life: 103
Having Integrity Be Your Foundation

CHAPTER 16

The Power of Forgiveness: From Suffering to Peace   107

CHAPTER 17

Creating Space for the Rest of Your Life: Forgiveness is the Key   117

CHAPTER 18

The Secret Key to Inventing Your Future: Taking a Stand   123

Part III: Awakening Your Sacred Listening for the World   139

CHAPTER 19

Stand-Taking as You Move through Life: Creating a New Future   141

CHAPTER 20

Creating a Sacred Listening for Life: Transforming Your   150
Relationship to Problems and Breakdowns

CHAPTER 21

Declaring Breakdowns as a Key to Breakthroughs: 156
From Expectation to Commitment

CHAPTER 22

Getting Interested in Getting Interested: Honoring Others   167

CHAPTER 23

Bringing Gratefulness, Faith, and Stand-Taking to a Crisis: 171
Making the Impossible Possible

Part IV: Awakening Your Sacred Listening for Spirit   179

CHAPTER 24

Finding my Thread: From Angst to Trusting Myself   181

CHAPTER 25

Leading a Life of True Joy: From Separateness to Belonging   189

CHAPTER 26

Becoming a Splendid Torch: Living from Service, Joy, and   204
Wholeheartedness

Afterword   *211*
Gratitudes   *213*
Notes   *222*
Permissions & Sources   *223*
Continue the Journey   *224*
About the Author   *226*

Foreword
By Lynne Twist

It is with great joy and deep respect that I introduce this luminous and life-giving book, *The Heart of Sacred Listening*, written by a woman I cherish as a beloved sister and soul companion on the path of awakening, transformation, and service.

For nearly fifty years, I have known Amba Gale to be a woman of profound integrity, unwavering purpose, and radiant love. From the earliest days of our friendship, I witnessed in her a fierce devotion to something greater than herself—the call to awaken human consciousness as the most essential act of healing for our planet and our times.

Amba's journey is one of depth and discipline. She immersed herself in the wisdom of many teachers and traditions, cultivating a practice of listening that became the foundation of her extraordinary gift: the ability to midwife transformation in individuals, organizations, and communities around the world. She is not only a teacher and coach—she is a guide, a poet, a mystic, and a master listener.

This book is a treasure. With grace, elegance, and unflinching honesty, Amba invites us into her own life—her successes and heartbreaks, her insights and revelations. She shares stories that are tender and true, teachings that are timely and timeless. Through it all, she offers us a profound invitation: to reclaim the sacred art of listening—not just to others, but to ourselves, to the Earth, to the invisible whispers of Spirit that guide our lives.

What I love about *The Heart of Sacred Listening* is how personal it is—and yet how universal. Amba writes with the warmth of a friend, the wisdom of a sage, and the rhythm of a poet. Whether she's describing the quiet courage required to face her husband's life-threatening illness or the insights gleaned from decades of transformational work, her words reflect heart, humility, and hope. Along with her insights about forgiveness, vulnerability, and turning breakdowns into breakthroughs, she offers practical advice and purposeful practices that connect you with your own wisdom and power.

Amba reminds us that listening is not a passive act—it is a courageous stance. To truly listen is to soften the ego, to welcome the unknown, to allow the world and one another to matter. It is a radical act of love. And love is at the heart of Amba's life and work.

At this critical moment in history—when the old paradigms are crumbling, and a new world is aching to be born—we are being asked to listen for messages and messengers we may not have heard before. As human supremacy gives way to human responsibility for the flourishing of all life, we seek guidance for a new path for humanity. Listening—to the Earth, to the Universe, to our own hearts—is fundamental to making this evolutionary leap. This book illuminates the inner journey that is necessary for our collective journey to a new future, and there could be no better time for its birth and presence on our planet.

The Heart of Sacred Listening will nourish your soul, uplift your spirit, and open your heart to what is possible. Savor its stories and practice its teachings. Let it be your companion as you navigate your own sacred journey.

Lynne Twist is a global visionary and proactivist committed to creating a future that is environmentally sustainable, spiritually fulfilling, and socially just. She is the co-founder of the Pachamama Alliance, the founder of the Soul of Money Institute, and author of *The Soul of Money* and *Living a Committed Life*. Her website is *soulofmoney.org*.

Blessings for You, the Reader

May *The Heart of Sacred Listening* be your teacher, your companion, and your guide for a while, as the path ahead calls to you to fulfill, as poet Mary Oliver says, your "one wild and precious life."

May you come into the rhythm of your heart's true longings, finding the extraordinary and the precious within your own core, touching the love and wisdom that lie within. From there, may you emerge into a new world; a world of your own creation.

May others be healed and enlivened by the sacredness of your Presence and your Listening.

May you welcome yourself—your True self—at a new door with joy and elation.

May you find your Self as your own inner teacher; your own Guide.

May you experience all that life has to offer you as a gift.

May you be surprised by who you are and what your life is meant to be at the end of this conversation.

May the Heart of Sacred Listening serve as a door to renewal, opening you into your next New Life.

Welcome to the Heart of Sacred Listening

I greet you in a perhaps peculiar kind of way. I greet you the way people in Eastern Tibet greet each other as they pass on those high mountain trails.

Similar to the more familiar "namaste," they bring their palms together in front of their chest, bow slightly, look into the other person's eyes, and say, "*Tashi Deley.*"

What does "*Tashi Deley*" mean?

It means, "I honor the greatness in you. I honor the place in your heart where lives your courage, honor, love, and dreams. I honor the place in you where if you are in that place in you and I am in that place in me, there is only one of us."

It is a beautiful greeting.

"*Tashi Deley.*"

Introduction

Have you ever wondered:

- How to talk so your kids will listen?
- How to talk so your boss will listen?
- Or your spouse will listen?
- Or your parents will listen? Your family? Or your co-workers? Your clients? Your teams?
- How to talk so that your relationships work?
- How to talk so you accomplish what you want?
- How to talk so that people in your business are productive, nourished, thriving, and collaborating well with each other?

Well, I have news for you.

You are asking the wrong question.

Real communication does not start with the question, "How do I 'talk' to another in a way that works?"

The real question is: How can we *listen* to one another in a way that works? I mean, *really* listen—provide deep, *sacred* listening.

Real Listening is rare and not so easy to come by.

We often find ourselves preoccupied with listening to our own thoughts, triggered feelings, and judgments while others speak. Or we are preparing what we will say when the other stops talking. Or we come from wanting to fix them rather than simply get their experience. Or we think we know what they will say before they are finished talking. So, we tune them out. Or, as Steve Martin says in one of his skits, "The Absent-Minded Waiter," we "go to the Bahamas" for a moment.

Real Listening, what I am calling Sacred Listening, is a pure gift. It is a gift you give to yourself, a gift you give to others, a gift you give to the world, a gift you may be blessed enough to receive from another. And it can be learned.

It is a gift that allows you to know you belong and that you are loved.

Desiring to know what it takes to really listen arises when you have the sense that there is another life that you could be living—one without the effort, the struggle, the sense of overwhelm, or the suffering. A life of fulfillment, meaning, freedom, and joy on an ongoing basis. A life in which your relationships, even those that currently don't work, work. A life in which you know you are making a difference.

Nearly everyone initially focuses on speaking—speaking well, speaking clearly, speaking confidently—as if speaking is the key to effective communication. However, the belief that communication primarily relies on speaking is a myth. Almost no one recognizes how crucial, essential, and vital listening is.

Have you noticed that in some conversations with people, you feel appreciated and understood, and experience a profound connection with them? You can tell how genuinely interested they are in you; sometimes, you even find yourself sharing things about your life that you would never open up to anyone else.

And then, in other conversations and communication relationships, you feel shut down and judged, and you can hardly speak?

That's why I say listening is vital. The word "vital" comes from Latin, meaning "of life, life-giving." Listening is life-giving.

Listening is the key to truly serving, to making a difference in another person's life. It opens the door to self-awareness and compassion.

That's a big deal. Why? Because, without self-awareness and compassion, when the world shows up as a threat to you, filled with competitors, enemies, and people who are up to no good, you act one way. If you are open-hearted, inclusive, and embracing, the world shows up as benign, generous, and abundant, one full of kindness and generosity, and you act another way.

Awakening your Heart Listening is the key to many doors, including heart-centered leadership, as you shift from not hearing to authentically and profoundly connecting with another. It is the key to successful relationships. It is the foundation for accomplishment. It opens space for you to create and then dance in a new world, one you were perhaps not dancing in before. Real listening, profound listening, allows you to listen to others, yourself, life, and the Greater Mystery through new ears and see through new eyes.

In this new world, your relationship with yourself and who you are—indeed, your own experience of yourself can be transformed. You can move from living from your head to living from your heart. You can move from living a life of struggle and resistance to living a life of joy and freedom. You can move from not wanting to be with certain people or merely tolerating them to creating empowering, loving, and life-changing relationships with them. You can move from thinking you are not worthy and don't matter very much to experiencing that you are making a meaningful and profound difference in the world.

You can open yourself up to a whole new perspective. Instead of feeling alone and possibly confused in a world where you try, drive, strive, and push your way through life to achieve a sense of success, you can embrace and develop a life in partnership, collaboration, and dialogue with others, where you generate ideas together that one person alone could never create.

Through listening with an awakened heart, life flows *through* you, not merely *by* you, and you're buoyed by the winds of spirit into a new future; a future of your own creation, rather than a future that is merely an extension of the past.

Through listening—real listening, which includes forgiving—you can heal yourself and others.

Through listening, you can shift from half-hearted living, living with a (proverbial) "foot out the back door," to embracing a life of passion, fully connected with your own Wisdom and Spirit.

Listening through your open and awakened heart, you can lead a meaningful, purposeful life in which your greatest gifts—the gifts you were born with—are expressed into and provided to a world that is hungry for them.

For forty years, I have worked with people to develop listening as a key to creating accomplishment. Contributing to organizations across various industries has shown me that fostering cooperation, communication, and collaboration frequently leads to unexpected breakthroughs. For example, in 2004, one of my clients, Parametrix, a research and development engineering firm in the Western United States, successfully reduced its attrition rate from 36 percent to 8 percent and maintained that low rate for many years by restoring trust in their workplace and sustaining it through time. You, too, can listen with your heart at home, within your business and work, and in your communities. From my decades of experience, I have observed that you can:

- Create and sustain relationships with your children, your spouse, your greater family, your business colleagues, that work and that enrich everyone

- Let go of limiting beliefs that lead to feelings of unworthiness or low self-esteem, resulting in a sense of self-empowerment, which naturally attracts other empowered people to you

- Have breakthroughs from breakdowns, and design a relationship with obstacles that come your way as life-giving rather than life-stopping

🔹 Lead a passionate, meaningful life; a life of joy that comes from being of service and knowing that you make a difference, and being freed up to make the difference that you are here to make

I am committed to *The Heart of Sacred Listening: The Key to Transforming Your Relationships, Your Work, and Your Life*, making a profound and lasting difference in your life. What will move that forward? What will pave the way for that to happen?

The clearer, more committed, and more specific you are in what you are "up to" while reading this book, the more power and impact it will have in your life.

I once had a coach who worked with me to make a difference in people's lives through coaching. He said, "If you can bring people to be at stake for something in their lives, something that really matters to them, you can read the phone book to them, and they will have a breakthrough!"

That's what I am committed to, for you: a breakthrough.

So, let us pause here before we get into our first story in order to maximize the opportunity for transformation in your life through reading this book.

I invite you to find a pen you love writing with. Choose any questions or questions that are relevant to you, or make up your own. Take a pause and address any of these questions, deliberately and intently:

What do you intend to gain by reading this book?

What is a shift, a new opening, or a possibility you would love to create for yourself?

What is your heart's deepest desire? What do you long for?

What would you like to move, change, create, or let go of in your life to lead a joyful, meaningful life?

Where are you feeling stuck, held back, or limited in life?

What new possibilities for building relationships—with yourself, with others, and with life—would you love to explore from here?

If you were to shift from "x" to "y," what would "x" be? What would "y" be?

What specific, personal areas, issues, or concerns would you like to impact in a meaningful, life-giving way? This could be in any domain—professional, personal, work-related, home-related, or community-related.

What are you passionate about that you feel some blockage around? If you experienced a breakthrough in this area, what difference would it make in your life?

I have structured this book in a particular way to maximize opportunities for the stories, teachings, and reflections to make a difference in your life. The book is divided into four parts.

Part I highlights distinctions, tools, and principles that allow you to create a breakthrough or transformation in your relationships with others by awakening the heart of listening.

Part II gives rise to a breakthrough in your relationship with yourself and in your own self-worth through that awakening.

Part III opens a new relationship with listening for Life and its many gifts, including the obstacles, challenges, and breakdowns we experience.

Part IV creates an opening for you to live a life of true joy, a life of meaning and purpose, a life where your spirit can soar, fulfilled, like the eagle.

Each part begins with a poem or prose that points to the essence residing at the heart of that transformation. Throughout the book, my own and others' real stories are included as inspirational examples—teachings for developing a compassionate, courageous, and generous heart, one that listens to life with sacred attention. Listening sacredly creates breakthroughs in life that would not otherwise occur.

Life-changing principles and distinctions are embedded within the stories and elaborated on later. You may experience "aha" moments as you read these stories.

What is personal can also be universal. That's your access to the experience that the stories offer. Please note that to achieve a level of practice or mastery in listening, you do not need to participate in any of the work I have done, or that I make available, or go on any particular similar adventures to mine. You just need to see where you connect with what is in the stories, and from there, reflect, become aware, and practice in action.

First, you may think you understand the distinctions I am drawing. But understanding alone is a "booby prize," and doesn't inspire you to make a difference in your own life. In school, understanding was important. But in the process of transformation, a different kind of learning happens. Inquiry is the key—not to find an answer but to "be with" a question that isn't easily answered. Reflection on the core of your own life experience becomes the teacher.

Picture a circle, like a pie. Let the pie represent the domain of knowledge. A slice of that pie, you could say, is what you know you know. When I was two years old, this slice covered the entire circle. Another slice is what you don't know you know. This slice of pie got larger as I got older. Then, there's another slice, one most people are unaware of. It's the slice of the pie called "What you don't know you don't know."

The territory in that slice is dark. So, first you grapple. Once you start to work with the principles and live from them, new possibilities begin to open for you in your life. As you continue to practice, you naturally begin to embody them, creating breakthroughs in your own life, your relationships, your work, and in life.

You'll notice, as you go, that I have included "stopping off" places called "Now It's Your Turn"—intentional pauses in the flow of the book where you can take a moment to stop, think, reflect, write, or journal about your own life, making the ideas of that chapter relevant to your own experience. If you choose to engage in this work, those pauses can last for any duration—a few minutes, an hour, a day, or even a week—whatever timing suits you best to begin embodying the tools and principles that can make a profound difference in your life.

The following classic story will get us started.

It was late at night. A man had dropped his car keys in the gutter. He frantically searched for them under the streetlamp. Another man came by. Seeing the man on his knees, looking for something, he asked, "What are you looking for? I'll help you find what you are looking for."

"I'm looking for my car keys," the first man said.

"Where did you lose them?"

The first man looked up at the man who was there to help and pointed to the gutter. "Over there, in the gutter," he said.

"Then why are you looking here?" the second man said.

"Because there's more light over here," the first man said.

We are always searching for the keys in the light. However, the vital keys to fulfilling a life are often lost in the darkness, where we can't easily see them. Finding those keys requires us to explore new, unfamiliar, and possibly uncomfortable territory. However, it is where the keys are, and this book will give you enough light.

The journey is well worth it.

PART I

Awakening Your Sacred Listening for Others

The Gift of Heart-Listening

Kokoro-to-Kokoro

Heart-listening and compassion are interwoven in such a marvelous way that they create a circle of caring. One gives rise to the other, and in turn is the result of the other. When we listen with the heart, we begin to feel compassion in a new way, and when we feel compassion, we also discover ourselves listening with the heart more spontaneously . . .

. . . The Japanese have a special phrase to describe this kind of heart-listening. They speak of kokoro-to-kokoro, which means "heart speaking to heart." For them, it is the most powerful form of communication because it is centered in love, and it is infallibly effective. They describe its effect as similar

to a stone dropped into a clear pool. It sends out ripples in ever-widening circles, until the farthest reaches of the shore are touched by its gentle waves. Heart-listening sends out waves of love that wash away the waste of negative emotions and usher in a new energy of compassionate caring.

Heart-listening is rare mainly because we have not understood the importance of it. We thus do not take the time to learn this beautiful and powerful art. Yet there seems to be a universal longing for this kind of communication. We want to be heard and understood by others at the deepest levels of our being. We want to be responded to with compassion. We all want to be in touch with the wisdom of our own hearts and be able to share this caring with others.

Wanting to learn this kind of listening is its essential prerequisite. By wanting, we open our hearts to the experience. It is not an art that is easily acquired. It demands discipline and attention and self-reflection, as well as the courage to take new risks. But the rewards are incredibly great for us and for those we touch with our listening.

The gift of heart-listening is, ultimately, the gift of our highest selves, and like all true gifts, one that enriches the giver as much as the receiver.

Andre Auw, Ph.D. *The Gift of Heart-Listening,* Chapter 2

CHAPTER 1

Who Am I?

The Question that Opened My Life

It was December 1972. I was twenty-seven years old, sitting in a banquet chair in the ballroom of the Jack Tarr Hotel in San Francisco with 200 others for a program that I had heard could transform my life. The handsome man at the front of the room, a man in his forties with brown, somewhat curly hair that spilled onto his forehead, had a booming voice and a charismatic presence was leading the program.

The previous year, I had passionately participated in weekend workshops at the Esalen Institute, an innovative center for humanistic psychology and personal development.

I had to do something. My identity crisis had started the year before.

Now, something amazing was happening in my life, and I wanted more of it.

Since graduating from the University of California, Berkeley, in 1968, I had been teaching high school English in a middle-to-upper-class neighborhood in the hills of Walnut Creek, California. There, I started a school within the school and won an award for innovative development from the California Teachers Association. I loved my job and the students.

When I was twenty-one, I married a man who was Jewish—all part of what my parents expected of me. Ever since I was a little girl, I knew I would get married at twenty-one.

He was perfect. He fit all the pictures. He had the right credentials. I had met him as a sophomore.

He was handsome. He had a great sense of humor. He was artistic. We had bought a home in the Montclair Hills with money I had inherited from my mother's passing. She had died of cancer when I was sixteen.

We had a living room with a fireplace and a deck overlooking the pine trees.

Life was perfect.

Well, not THAT perfect. And I knew it. I didn't want to know it, but I knew it.

One night, he didn't come home. Then the next night, he still didn't come home. And after that, the same happened again. He had found someone else to spend his nights with.

We were not content in our relationship anyway, and it shouldn't have been a surprise, but it was.

Six months later, we got a divorce—quite an amicable divorce. Once the initial crisis passed, we remained friends. That crisis ultimately became the opportunity my soul was longing for—to break free and go deep.

The Chinese ideogram for crisis is the same ideogram for opportunity. That certainly was the case here, as a new life opened for me in the letting go of the old.

However, at the time, I felt like a tsunami of *I am not loved* swept over me from my past, my present, and all of my future. I felt ungrounded, at sea without a lifeboat, lost. I was drowning, tossed about by surface waves of turbulence.

Worst of all, I didn't know who I was without the role of wife.

It was a surprise to me to find myself so lost, without the roles and without the ways I had been defining myself.

I had been a wife, a teacher, a good girl, a daughter who obeyed her parents, and a good student. However, I realized that those were only roles, distinct from who I was.

That critical, crucial, essential question, "Who am I?" became a guiding force in my life.

At first, I felt like a child lost in a thick forest of redwoods without a map, a trail of breadcrumbs, or a canteen. Later, as I began to explore, inhabit, and live in that question, it became inspiring, enlivening, and a source of passionate living.

As I began to journey inside that question, I realized that many other people were living with the same question.

You might be living with that question.

I devoured books I had never read before. Ram Das's *Be Here Now* was profound, awakening. So was Alan Watts's *The Book*. So was Adi Da's *Knee of Listening*, Paramahansa Yogananda's *Autobiography of a Yogi*, and Suzuki's *Zen Mind, Beginner's Mind*. All freed up my thinking, opening me into new territory to explore and think within.

I began journeying to the Big Sur coast every weekend, a four-hour drive away. I looked forward to my weekly pilgrimage to The Esalen Institute. This remote, burgeoning institute for human awareness, personal growth, and self-exploration exists outside of time, perched on a high cliff where the waves continuously crash against the rocky shore below, akin to Beethoven's "Ode to Joy," evoking timeless themes of mystical, musical, and magical wonder. I heard the waves in the background constantly—at night, on walks to the hot baths, on the trails, and even in my sleep.

I relished being with transformative teachers, philosophers, and psychologists.

I immersed myself in workshops every weekend, exploring various disciplines such as Gestalt therapy, aikido, Rolfing, psychodrama, sensory awareness, meditation, and Tai Chi. It was wonderful, delicious, and divine.

And the question, "Who am I?" began to become increasingly exciting. I met so many other people who were living inside that same exploration. The question evolved from being rooted in fear to becoming exciting, then transforming into an opening, ultimately serving as a path to awakening.

And now, in December of that year, I was with two hundred people in a training to find out who I was. Sitting in that director's chair on stage in that hotel ballroom was the charismatic founder of *est* (for the Latin, "to be") in front of me. He had a booming voice and was a straight shooter. His training represented the next step in my path.

With many of the other participants sharing their own stories, I was moved, and I felt safe. I saw things about myself I had never seen before, and I gained insights and realizations. I saw how I blamed others when things "went wrong" or how I held on to resentments for a long time.

I also saw that I wanted to give myself a full-blown immersion, more than just on weekends, dedicating my life to exploration. I wanted to profoundly devote myself to the inner work, to "acquiring" self-awareness. I wanted to identify the patterns that were holding me back, patterns I hadn't even realized were limiting me. I wanted to wake up!

I wanted to take a full year's leave from teaching.

I wanted to give myself the blessing of a life filled with exploring that question, meeting others on the path to "enlightenment" or "awakening," discovering my purpose, and living a life of meaning, passion, freedom, and joy.

As I contemplated taking that leave, I suddenly heard an inner, admonishing voice say, *You can't take a leave of absence because Daddy won't let you.*

I knew I couldn't. I just couldn't see or act on that possibility because Daddy wouldn't let me.

The voice was sharp, punitive, angry, admonishing, severe, and instilled fear.

Huh? I argued to myself. *I'm twenty-seven years old. I am an adult. I can do what I want with my life.*

A dialogue ensued.

Well, it wasn't a dialogue. It came back to one repeating admonishment, like a hellish mantra: *Yes, I know, but Daddy still won't let you.*

Daddy won't let you. Daddy won't let you. Daddy won't let you, echoed down dark hallways of my mind.

CHAPTER 2

My Dad and I

From Resistance to Love

I came to a complete stop. Werner Erhard, the "trainer," or leader and founder of the program, asked us to look and see what story we were living in with respect to the issue we were dealing with.

My story about my dad was clear to me: he was a controller, a manipulator, old-fashioned, out to make you do whatever *he* wanted you to do.

And I had plenty of evidence for that. I was sure of that. There was no question about that. I had seen that all my life.

I had plenty of evidence.

As a student, if I came home with five As and a B, he'd scowl, "What about the B?"

As soon as I came home from school, I *had* to spend two hours a day practicing piano, even when I didn't want to. For eight years.

My other friends were hanging out in the afternoon. I felt sorry for myself, like a victim of my parents' demands. After all, though, I was a "good girl," and I would not dare go against their wishes.

During my senior year of high school, I fell in love with someone who was not Jewish. My parents did not want me to see him. I saw him anyway. While some of the things we did together, they knew about it, some they didn't. They weren't happy about that relationship at all.

I always had a curfew of 10:00 p.m., even during my senior year of high school. I remember that my best friend Naomi once had a "make-out party," when several couples got together and they all "made out" (an old term for kissing). Naomi's parents, quite liberal, were at the back of the house.

So, there we were, the lights way down low, and Johnny Mathis's "Chances Are" was playing on the phonograph. It was around 10:00 p.m.

There was a loud thump on the front door. Very loud. We all straightened up. Naomi stopped the record. She turned the lights up. She opened the door.

It was my dad who came to take me home. He was angry.

I was embarrassed and humiliated.

Now, eleven years later, sitting in my seat in that hotel room, I remembered all of this.

Werner asked us to do one thing: run a movie of our lives, examining all the evidence that proved I was right about the story I was living, that validated my own listening,—that my father's intention was to control me—and find *another* interpretation or another narrative that accounted for the same evidence (without changing the evidence) but came into a story that served and empowered.

To drop one story and invent another, one that would be more life-giving.

I did that. I played that movie over and over and over and over again in my mind. I was dedicated to seeing something new. I was committed. I was sweating. I was uncomfortable. I just kept seeing a dad who was out to control my life. I just knew that I was right about him.

There was one problem: I had been living my life as a victim, with him as the persecutor and controller, leaving me with no say in my own life. Now, I wanted to break free and create a life that would allow me to fulfill something bigger, something more meaningful, more substantial, and more enlivening. I aimed to live a well-lived life. So, I intentionally sought a new story with a great deal of commitment and dedication.

And then, suddenly, I had an epiphany.

I realized that if I had led the same life my father had—if I had grown up where he had grown up, had the life experiences he had, been enculturated the same way he had, seen how to succeed like he did, having grown up in another generation—the generation he grew up in—*I would have been exactly the same way.*

My father was born in Ukraine, in a little Jewish shtetl (Ital shtetl)—a small village—south of Kyiv. He had three brothers and three sisters. His father held a leadership position over transportation into and out of Berdichev, which was on the main train line. Because of his position, he had some prominence in the town. He was murdered along with other leaders by the Cossacks. The two older brothers immigrated to Canada, and the third brother to Los Angeles. My father immigrated with his mother when he was fourteen. The three sisters were all married and stayed in Berdichev. During the Depression, Dad lived with one of his brothers in New York, in the garment district, doing hard work for a living.

Eventually, years later, he was accepted into the Illinois Institute of Technology, working many hours while studying to earn a mechanical engineer's license. His experience taught him that education is everything, that having a serious work ethic matters, and that focus is crucial.

His wife, my mother, faced cancer twice, which was a huge struggle for both of them and, of course, her suffering impacted my world. She ultimately died of cancer when I was sixteen after four years of fighting the disease.

Then he was a single parent, to me, a strong, high-spirited, and headstrong only daughter who was resistant to him most of the time. I did not want to listen.

Yet, all he wanted was to contribute to my happiness and prevent me from suffering. He wanted me to have a good life, a successful life, a productive life.

That realization—that there was a different way of looking at it all— allowed me to create an entirely different set of eyes and ears. Compassion opened within me and brought me close to him. The world had changed suddenly, and so had my relationship with my father.

I saw that all he *really* wanted, out of his love for me, his only daughter, who he had virtually raised by himself since I was twelve, as my mother was dying from cancer for four years during that time, was to contribute to my happiness.

My brain exploded.

Everything looked different: my relationship with my father, my relationship with the world, and my relationship with myself.

I felt like I had just made a slight turn in the kaleidoscope of life from "all he wants to do is to manipulate me" to "all he wants to do is contribute to my happiness," and the shapes and colors of my life were all different.

My heart opened. I wept.

The world was born anew.

Suddenly, I was freed up. At the exact moment that the refreshing, purifying rains of revelation washed through my mind and opened my heart, I also realized that I would be taking a year off from teaching. I had no question about it.

I was free.

You might say that *I listened to my father in a different way*, or that I had a different father—a different life.

He went from being a man who only wanted to control me to being a man who wanted, more than anything, to contribute to my happiness.

I didn't need to resist him if I could listen for his contribution to me. I could climb into his shoes and consider what he saw from his point of view. I could be open instead of closed.

In one instant, the world shifted from adversary to partnership, from scarcity to abundance, and from fear to love. That's called transformation.

CHAPTER 3

Transforming My Relationship With My Father

The Gift of Heart Listening

I was excited about this revelation and wanted to get on a plane immediately and see my father. But I didn't. I wanted to talk with him right away, not wait for a plane flight.

I was going to apologize to him for how and who I had been for so many years, for being resistant to him. It must have been incredibly hard for him, and I wanted to acknowledge that and mend our relationship.

I wanted to share with him what I had discovered about his orientation for my life.

I wanted to tell him I was taking a leave of absence from teaching. Although I didn't think he'd like it, I was committed to completing whatever we needed to do to make that happen.

Before I got on the phone call with him, I did something smart: I wrote down a prompt for myself on a piece of paper, a question. And I vowed to myself that I would not engage with him unless I could say "yes" to the question. I knew that if I were talking to a controller or a manipulator, things were not going to go well. If I could speak with my dad as someone who genuinely cared about my happiness, the conversation would work.

The question I wrote down was: "Can you hear his commitment to your happiness?" And I promised myself I would not speak unless I could hear that commitment.

I called Dad first thing the next morning. I could hear the phone ringing in his house, the house I grew up in. I was excited and nervous at the same time. "How was the course?" he asked me, early into the call.

"Are you sitting down?" I asked him.

He said, "No, but I will."

He knew something was up and that whatever I had to say was something important.

I began with a profound apology, from my heart, and I truly meant it.

I told him I was sorry for being so resistant for so long during my teenage years when he was a single parent; that I could only imagine how challenging that must have been for him. I told him that I recognized that I was headstrong and had my own perspective, which made me feel like he was trying to control me.

I told him that I made a huge discovery—that all he ever wanted was to contribute to my happiness, to see me strong, to support me in fulfilling my potential, and to be the kind of person he knew I could be.

He was still. Quiet. For a long time.

Then, I could hear him weep. He must have wept for five minutes. I hung in there with him. When he could speak again, he said, "That's all I have ever wanted for you, Marilyn." (Yes, that's the name he and Mom gave me.) "That's all I've *ever* wanted. And I thought I was going to have to die and go to my grave without you ever, ever knowing this. This has made me so happy."

I suddenly understood his reality: that my Dad thought he would have to die without my knowing the depth of his care and his love.

I realized even more deeply how astonishing that transformation was.

We celebrated a little together, peacefully. We were both happy.

And then, he was ready to say goodbye to me.

I said, "Well, before we get off this call, here's one more thing."

"Oh? What's that?" he said, curious, excited, and vitally interested.

I took a deep breath. "I've decided to take a leave of absence from teaching for a year."

All hell broke loose.

"YOU'RE GOING TO DO **WHAT?**"

I told him again.

"I have heard you say some crazy things, but this is THE CRAZIEST thing I've ever heard you say."

That's the last thing I heard him say for quite a while. I shut down. My heart withdrew from the conversation. I stopped listening.

And then he started yelling at me. Since I wasn't listening, I don't even know what he said. All I knew was that my own, loud, internal voice had kicked in. *He can't talk to you like that! You are an adult! You are twenty-seven years old, and you can do whatever you want with your life!*

He became for me, once again, "the controller, the jailer, and the enemy."

Angry and resistant, I was about to say, "Hey! I am an adult! I can do whatever I want with my life."

Then, I read those words on my piece of paper: "Can you hear his commitment to your happiness?"

I knew the answer was no, so I kept my mouth shut.

He kept yelling. I started to give up. *Okay*, my internal voice said, with a sigh of resignation, *I'll do whatever you want me to do. I won't go on that leave.*

I almost said it. I almost said, "OKAY, I won't go."

Then I looked at my piece of paper and asked myself, *Can you hear his commitment to your happiness?* And I knew the answer was still "no."

He kept on yelling. I had no idea what he was saying.

I knew I had some work to do.

I knew I needed to let go of the story I had been living in for so many years—one that was so disempowering to me, to him, and to our relationship. I knew I had to "shift my listening" to hear his passion, to listen to the "why" behind his being so upset. Whatever he was saying, he meant it, and I knew he meant it. And I couldn't hear it.

With all my heart, guts, commitment, and desire, I shifted the location of my attention from listening to my own voice inside of me (at this point, it was the "give in" voice) to *locating* myself with him. I put myself, my energy, my attention, and my presence over there, with him, profoundly committed to hearing his own commitment to contribute to my happiness.

Finally, when I shifted my listening, I finally shifted my world.

I became another person, and so did he.

I was interested—beyond curious—in what my father had to say to me and in what contribution he wanted to make to me. He was someone who wanted to contribute to his daughter's happiness.

Suddenly, I was calm and present for whatever he had to say to me without resistance. I could hear his words and his concern for me. I was no longer defensive, protective, resigned, or a victim. I was committed to being contributed to by him, and I listened *for* his contribution.

A new world opened once I could listen.

So, I asked him, interested, wanting to know, "What is so concerning to you? What are you worried about? What do you see that I don't see? I want to understand."

Once I shifted, so did he. He now had a daughter who wanted to hear what he had to say.

He said he thought it might be the right move, but at the wrong time. I was going through a divorce, and my whole life was destabilized. He reminded me that I love teaching and that I love my students. I felt safe and secure in teaching, that this was *not* the time to invent a new life, to explore, or to go on an adventure.

I could understand that viewpoint and how much sense it made—I really could. Had it occurred six months earlier, it would have been good advice, which I probably would have followed.

What my dad didn't know was that I had already stepped way out. I was in unknown territory and loving it, even if it was not "safe" in the usual sense of that word. I had given myself the opportunity to explore and start to become self-aware. I was looking for those lost keys. Telling the truth to myself about myself was safe enough. I wanted to be out on my own, in the unknown, so I could further explore, awaken, and distinguish who I was and what I was meant to do with my life in this new world, without any familiar structures to confine me or define me.

I shared that with him. And he got it. The energy shifted.

Not only did he understand, but he was genuinely glad to hear it, and he became curious himself. Once he had stopped and absorbed what I was saying, he asked me if I knew what I was going to do next in my life.

I did know.

Back then, John Denver's "Rocky Mountain High" was my favorite song. I, too, was twenty-seven, and I felt like I had come home to myself. I also discovered the keys to creating a life that worked. And, having grown up in Los Angeles and then lived in the Berkeley area, I had never lived in the mountains. I loved the mountains! My parents used to take me to Yosemite when I was a child, and it was, and still is, my favorite place to go. I had a hunger to live in the mountains.

I told him I wanted to move to the Colorado Rockies.

My father was quiet for a few moments. I could tell he was absorbing that and then thinking about that. When he spoke, he sounded intrigued: "Wow," he said. "Ever since I was a young boy growing up in the Soviet Union, I've always wanted to be in the pine trees, especially during the winter, when it snows at night. The icicles hang from the trees in the morning, and as the sun rises, they create beautiful, colorful prisms. That will be so wonderful for you. Do you think I might come up and visit you?"

A year later, he did visit me. Even in the uninsulated cabin at the 10,000-foot level, with only a small wood-burning stove, it was wonderful.

That conversation marked the beginning of my life of freedom, my life of awakening—a life where I have had the privilege of making a difference in the lives of so many people.

Soon thereafter, I took a forty-day training program called Arica, which drew from many eclectic paths. I became an Arica trainer, continued my work with *est*, the educational institution that had contributed so much to my awakening, and moved to Boulder.

The following summer, I met Baba Muktananda, a renowned Indian guru, who gave me my new name: Amba. There is a great Hindu legend about her, which I will share with you in Chapter 24 of this book. Baba became an essential part of my life and my awakening.

Next, we will look beneath the transformation with my father to discover the essential tools of the Heart of Sacred Listening—tools that make wholeness, healing, and power possible.

But before we turn there, the next chapter offers a brief interlude of reflection. I invite you to explore a few questions designed to deepen your engagement and open the way for your own breakthroughs.

CHAPTER 4

Making this Your Own

Setting Yourself up for a Breakthrough

The various sections of our book offer you, as author Andre Auw suggests, the opportunity to "learn this kind of listening." We first learn by "wanting." We must desire deeply, for as Auw states, "It demands discipline and attention and self-reflection, as well as the courage to take new risks. But the rewards are incredibly great for us and for those we touch with our listening."

While I shared an extraordinary breakthrough in my life with my father, the true opportunity of this book and its stories is to encourage you to dive deeper, beyond the narratives, to discover the underlying principles at work, allowing you to apply and practice them in your own life.

Do you have a relationship, like the one I had with my dad, that just doesn't seem to be working? It might be someone important to you. It may even be someone with whom you are not very close, such as a coworker or colleague you struggle to get along with. If you are a teacher, it could be a student. If you are a mother, it might be your teenager. If you are a doctor, it could be a patient you hold dear.

What's a relationship you would like to open up? Or where do you want to move forward, but feel blocked by a specific relationship with someone in your life? Think about that. Take some time. The opportunity here is to make this real in your own life.

Okay. Do you have someone in mind? If you don't, just keep thinking. Good.

If you haven't already, consider creating a journal to accompany your inner travels as you read this book. A favorite pen, one that holds special meaning for you or that you enjoy writing with, could also be supportive. I know that when I write in the mornings, I love using a special pen. However, that's entirely up to you. That's how I would engage with the opportunity if I were just starting this book.

Here's the first question, and it's a question to ponder and tell the truth about: What is it costing you to keep that relationship stuck? A cost is something you are paying out. What is your cost? Your happiness? Your peace? Your well-being? Name that cost.

I invite you to stop and think. Maybe write. Take your time. And when you are ready, here is the second question: What new possibility might open up for you if that relationship were to get unstuck? Allow yourself to imagine the possibility!

Here's a secret: the deeper your interest in a breakthrough in your own life, the stronger your commitment to it, the more likely it is to happen. I call it "longing for." A profound longing for. A commitment. A "no matter what" kind of longing for. The deeper your longing, the stronger your commitment, the greater the chance of a breakthrough. Why? Because you are listening to the conversation differently, or reading the words intently, shifting from casual listening or "wouldn't that be nice" listening to "at stake" listening.

With my dad, at a certain moment, I realized that I was committed to taking that leave of absence to free myself up. The future of my very life was at stake, and while I couldn't see the shapes and forms, I had a clear sense that only by creating that kind of space for myself—space for exploration, discovery, reflection, and stepping onto new, unfamiliar ground—would the far horizon that was calling to me begin to take shape, and the keys start to reveal their locations.

So, with that longing in mind, that person in mind, and with that breakthrough in mind, let us begin. Like Frodo, and with a sense of great adventure, let us leave the Shire.

CHAPTER 5

"Files"

The Stories We Tell Ourselves

There are three great mysteries in life:
Air to a bird, water to a fish, and man to himself.
—an old Hindu riddle

What makes water a mystery to a fish?

If you take a pause and think about it, you will see that what makes water a mystery to a fish is that *the fish doesn't know it's swimming in water*. For the fish to know he's swimming in water, what must happen?

That's right: you would have to take the fish out of the water!

So now we are going to take ourselves out of our own water.

Imagine this scenario:

It's your first day at your new workplace. You are excited. You've gone through the interview process. You like the culture of the company, you like the people, you like the values, and you are looking forward to being a participative and enthusiastic member of this company. You can hardly wait to meet the people you will be working with, hopefully, for a long, long time.

You are warmly greeted by people who shake your hand and welcome you all morning.

Then, something surprising happens. It's around 11:00 a.m. Someone is coming toward you with their head down, moving quickly. Unlike most other people, who have had their hand extended for a greeting, this person, let's call her Sarah, doesn't even look up. She just walks on by without even acknowledging your presence.

Unbeknownst to you, Sarah's boss has just informed her that she must cancel the vacation with her family that she was looking forward to next week. Sarah is not only unhappy; she is also upset and angry.

So, Sarah passes you without saying hello.

What do you do?

You say to yourself, *Humph! I think her name is Sarah. Sarah isn't very friendly.*

You take out an imaginary manila file, write Sarah's name on it, and drop your decision of "not very friendly" inside the folder. Then you go on with your morning.

Later that morning, you're standing around the water cooler with another person, let's call her Joyce. Joyce asks you how your morning has been. You say flatly, "Fine."

The "fine" is not wholehearted or happy. Joyce picks up on the subtext. She wants to know if people have welcomed you. You say yes, you have. She wants to know if anything happened that made you feel uneasy about the company.

You remember the incident with Sarah. When you ask Joyce if she knows Sarah, she enthusiastically says, "Yes, I know Sarah." "Well, Sarah's not very friendly, is she?"

Joyce wrinkles her brows, confused. "Hmm," she says. "I never thought that."

And then she stops, and starts thinking . . . and thinking, and thinking, and thinking, and she says, "Now that I think about it, you know what? About fifteen years ago, there was a company picnic, and you know what happened at the picnic?"

She proceeds to tell a story about Sarah, which illustrates that perhaps she's not so friendly after all.

What do you do? You take out your invisible manila file on Sarah and put the evidence Joyce just gave you into it. And now your file is a little thicker, a little heavier, a little more real than it was before Joyce spoke. And Joyce, who did not have a file on Sarah before your own decision about her, now takes out a file on Sarah.

And here's the nasty part about this, the unseen part, the part that kills life:

Sarah, a talented, committed, and passionate individual eager to make a difference in her company, now has fewer opportunities to thrive there than she did before that little conversation (which was a big conversation). She has less chance of finding happiness and fewer opportunities to build relationships with others in her workplace.

You could say that she now has to live in a communication environment that is based on someone's opinion, someone's judgment, someone's conclusions, and someone's story. You could say she has "less listening."

Let me take a brief interlude from our story here.

What just happened is called "gossip."

What does gossip do?

Gossip creates realities that are based on no possibility. Gossip creates a negative listening, as it is subtly undermining, belittling, and cutting.

What is it?

It occurs when two or more people discuss a third person in a way that diminishes the listening for the third person in their eyes, without anyone addressing that third person directly.

You could think of gossip as a disease that erodes the vitality of a business or any relationship. It creates false realities; it undermines, belittles, and deadens.

Gossip has the effect of having some past judgment extend forward into the present and the future.

"How do I stop gossip?" you might ask.

Well, one way is: simply don't listen.

Another way is to stop doing it yourself.

Sometimes, we may not want to take this route, because if a relationship is built on gossip, it might feel like you're disrupting its foundation. If that's the case, here's what you can say to interrupt the gossip pattern without jeopardizing the relationship: *I realized, recently, how destructive gossip is, and I know you and I have been gossiping about this person and that person for quite a while now. And I'm going to stop doing that. It doesn't mean I care for you any less; it's just not productive. I am now going to go talk to her or him directly and communicate whatever I am feeling.*

> *I am also going to stop listening to gossip. So, I want to ask for your support in this: if I ever start gossiping to you again, would you please remind me that I made a promise to stop that and redirect me? Good. If I hear you start gossiping to me, I will ask you to speak to that person directly.*
>
> *Are you good with this?*

I have seen it over and over and over in organizations with which I've worked: when gossip stops, trust builds. And trust is everything.

Now, imagine it's the next day. The company has experienced a shift in thinking, and Sarah's vacation has been restored. She is now her true self and can simply "be." She can be present. She is no longer in her head, feeling upset. She sees you and warmly extends her hand to greet you.

Do you extend yours back? No! You are hesitant to do so. Not just hesitant. You don't want to! Why?

Because once you are in a story and you believe that story, all the evidence then has to fit in with that story. Why? To prove you're right. So, while you may, in a lukewarm way, meet Sarah, what you are thinking to yourself is something like this:

She's a manipulator. She gets friendly when she wants something from you.

—or some version of that. And that goes into the file, as well.

And now the file is a little thicker; a little more substantial.

What do we do? We distort the data to fit the story we invented and now believe. We distort the data to fit the paradigm. The evidence has to "fit in."

So, a vicious circle occurs. There's something that happens, then there's a reaction to that something, like disappointment or hurt, and then we create our story, and then the story gets confused with the event. We can no longer pry them apart.

And we become the story. We become one with that belief, and we stay stuck in that belief. And we don't even see anything that contradicts that belief. You could say, we "listen" *through* that belief.

Here is an anecdotal story I heard somewhere:

A newlywed couple moved into a new neighborhood. During breakfast, the young woman looked out the window and saw her neighbor hanging her laundry to dry. She commented to her husband how dirty the laundry was and said perhaps she needed better soap.

Her husband didn't say anything. For the next few weeks, every time the neighbor hung her laundry to dry, she made the same remark to her husband. She even asked him to go over there and show her how to do the laundry. He didn't know how to respond to her, so he just kept silent. This continued for weeks.

Then, one day, the woman looked out and saw a beautiful, clean, white wash hanging on the line. She remarked to her husband how amazing it was, as she had clearly learned how to wash.

Finally, the newlywed husband tapped into his own courage and said to her, "I got up early this morning and cleaned our windows."

You and I see through dirty windows. I call them "files."

A good way to engage this next part is to "consider the possibility." Your own mind may come up with *but, but, but . . .* because this is the part people don't really like to get. So, watch your mind! And every time your mind comes up with *but, but, but* or *that may be true for her, but not for me*, just thank your mind for sharing with you, and come back and consider the possibility of what I am saying.

1. We are constantly creating files, unknowingly. We live in those files, those stories, those beliefs, and those interpretations. They are the "dirty windows" we look through.
2. We have files on everyone.
3. We confuse the event, or what occurred, with our story *about* the event. And that story or belief now shapes what we see (or shapes our perception), and that shaping validates our story.
4. We live in our stories; our files. We live in the reality that *she's not very friendly*, and we don't notice that this is a story distinct from the event, e.g., *she walked by me with her head down.*

So, let's break it down into steps.

Step One:

Am I willing to *consider the possibility* that the story I am living in is shaping my perception?

And: What is the story?

Am I willing to consider the possibility that I am looking through a dirty window?

Here's a sidebar: my dad had glaucoma. He had to wear dark glasses whenever he was outdoors. One day, my husband Don and I took him to a nice restaurant in Santa Monica. The atmosphere was somewhat muted, with dark wood walls. My dad walked in and asked why we would take him to such a dingy place. I looked at him and told him he had his sunglasses on. He took them off. "OH!" he said, looking around. "This is really nice!"

Step Two:

Shift the question.

The question is *not* "is this true?" or "Am I right?" but:

Does this story, this belief, this *structure of interpretation* empower or disempower? Does it expand or constrain? Forward connection or forward disconnection?

Be ruthless with yourself. Tell the truth.

Step Three:

If it hurts or feels disempowering, let it go. It's possible that forgiveness will need to come into play, and we will dive into the pure waters of that particular healing balm later.

For now, don't let go of the event—after all, the event happened—but let go of your judgment or story. Own that it's your reactivation that's running the show, and create a new structure of interpretation that can account for the same event.

As an example, revisiting the story of my dad and me, I shifted from *he's out to control, dominate, and manipulate me,* to *he's out to contribute to my happiness.* Same events, but the shift in perspective through which I was listening made all the difference in our relationship and in how that conversation unfolded in the world.

The files themselves are rooted in a paradigm of right or wrong.

One of the most pervasive, habitual ways of being in life, of listening, is through the paradigm of right or wrong.

Just as a coffee maker makes coffee or a lawn mower cuts grass, a human being makes themselves right and others wrong.

It's built into our design; it's hard-wired. This is the mind's job.

Let's call it "the survival mind." Engaging in life through right or wrong is somehow connected to our survival, our identity, or, you could say, the survival of our identities, which is who we consider ourselves to be.

How does it occur? For example, it occurs as *blame.* "It's their fault. It's because of them, those jerks."

Once you see a file *just as a file,* or view a story only as a story, and recognize your blame, antagonism, or judgment as a triggered response, you can free yourself from it; that structure of interpretation no longer confines you.

In the video *The Business of Paradigms: Discovering the Future,* futurist Joel Barker says,

> *Once you see a paradigm, you can choose to shrug off one paradigm and adopt another: you can choose to see the world anew.*

So I invite you to get out the shredder!

Shred those files!

He also says, "We must be ready to recognize our current paradigms and go beyond them."

Paradigms shape our perceptions.

You can see the practical value: if the world appears to you as a threat, you act one way—you defend and protect yourself while keeping your heart hidden. If it occurs as benign, friendly, or an opportunity, you approach it unencumbered and open.

Again, from Barker:

> We see best what we're supposed to see. And poorly, or not at all, that data that doesn't fit our paradigm and see not at all what doesn't fit our paradigm.

I love this one:

> To her lover, a beautiful woman is a delight;
> To a monk, she's a distraction;
> To a mosquito, a good meal.
>
> Tara Bennett-Goleman

It appears that we see what is out there. However, what is really happening is it's my perspective, my story, my belief that has interpreted the world to be a certain way.

If I shift my story, I change my perception.

You can reperceive the world. Reperceiving the world allows you to shift your relationship to that world.

Step Four (and this one is a doozy):

We need to point the finger in our own direction, looking to ourselves first. It automatically goes squarely outward, to blame the big, bad "THEY." "If they'd only . . ."

When you point the finger in your own direction, you are asking the following question: "Am I willing to consider the possibility that I have something to do with how the world occurs to me?"

I didn't say this is easy . . . this can be hard!

Are we willing to say: "I am the author of my story that I am living in!"

You can stop, pause, and think for as long as you'd like.

You can say, "It's my listening that makes the world appear a certain way."

When we are in the market for buying a house, we could say we are "Listening for houses for sale." Don't we, then, notice "For Sale" signs everywhere?

How are you doing so far?

Okay.

If you think about it, this is both good news and bad news.

The good news is that listening is malleable. It's changeable. It's not fixed.

If the world is rigid and fixed and you are merely an innocent observer reporting on "the truth," you are left with very few options, none of which work: change another, fix another, isolate them, manipulate them, avoid them, gossip and undermine them, or leave them. But if perception is a function of your listening, you can shift your listening, or "you can choose to see the world anew," as Barker says.

The bad news is . . . (are you ready for it? You are probably not going to like it.)

The bad news is: you have to give up your addiction to being right, give up being off the hook, give up your blame, excuses, and feeling sorry for yourself; you have to let all of that go!

I am not suggesting that you ignore the data. This is not positive thinking or "putting whipped cream on top of garbage," as Bob Hoffman, founder of the deeply healing Hoffman Quadrinity Process, says.

I am saying we tend to take our interpretations as facts. And we know that we're right!

I am suggesting that you learn to separate the data, the facts, or the observable events from your structures of interpretation and know that your interpretations are just that—interpretations! *Oh! That's a fact, and that's an interpretation!* Facts are distinct from assessments, stories, and interpretations.

If you continue to hang on to your story or interpretations, you can continue to be "right." And you will continue to have evidence (and agreement) for your point of view. You can't underestimate the pull of being right.

Again, the question is not *Am I right?* but *Does this structure of interpretation help or hinder, empower or disempower, free or constrict our ability to work together and accomplish what we intend?*

I am not saying not to interpret the things that happen to you. I am simply advising you to ask yourself: *Does this interpretation empower me, others, or the business?*

You can also ask yourself, *What is it costing me to be right?*

Seriously. I invite you to examine that question. Dig deep into that question. It frequently costs us our well-being. It can cost us our happiness, and it certainly can and does cost us our relationships.

What's the cost?

Many gravestones could bear this phrase: "I died, but I was right!"

Engaging in action with another person from a place of honor, compassion, and attentive listening to their brilliance and wisdom will lead to a very different kind of conversation than if you approach them from a pre-existing "file" or story.

So, let me give you another example from my own life.

I worked as an independent consultant and coach with Hewlett-Packard for about twenty years. At the start of one of the courses I was leading, an in-house course for HP engineers, one of the engineers faced a tough decision: whether to fire a team member. His relationship with that employee had been poor. He was fed up and planned to use the course to decide whether to fire him and, if so, how to have that conversation.

I asked him to tell me about it.

He said, "All he wants to do is waste my time."

I asked him if that was a story or a fact. He said it was a fact.

I asked him to tell me about the event—to explain what happened when he engaged with that employee. He said, "I just told you. Every day he comes into my office, he wastes my time."

This went on for quite a while. He just couldn't get that it was a story.

Now this was an engineer from HP; no dummy.

After about ten to fifteen minutes of working with him to tell me the facts, he finally understood what I was asking.

"Oh," he said. "He comes into my office and speaks loudly every day, complaining."

I asked him what the engineer was complaining about. He didn't know. He didn't know because he didn't listen. After all, he knew this guy was just going to waste his time. Why listen?

I said to him, "You know? Complainers are often passionate people who want to make a difference but think they won't be heard or listened to, so they speak loudly. They are people who are often disappointed and turn cynical because they don't want to be disappointed again."

The engineer got it. He promised himself he would listen to the complainer's commitment to make a difference when next he was with him.

After our group's three-week break, he returned to class and raised his hand to share.

He said, "The next day after we spoke, I was in my office, and that guy came in and started wasting my time. I was disgusted. I said to myself, 'See? He didn't get it.' Then I realized I was the one who had taken the course, not him!

"And I stopped. I changed my tone. I apologized to him. I let him know I had become aware that he had something to say, and had for a long time, and that I had not been listening.

"And I promised him I'd listen."

He then said to his classmates, his fellow engineers, "Do you remember when I moved that piece of equipment on the fabrication floor from one area to the opposite area, which saved us $250,000 that first week?"

Everyone nodded.

"That was his idea. It came out of my meeting with that person."

That story ultimately transformed the entire team's listening for each other. That example contributed to the development of an integrated and effective team.

Partnership, collaboration, integration, trust, and *listening* were born.

Making This Your Own

> *Every man takes the limits of his own*
> *field of vision for the limits of the world."*
> —Arthur Schopenhauer

If you completed the work at the end of Chapter 4, you brought someone into your mind's presence.

While reading this chapter, you may have noticed that you have files on that person. What are they?

And what are the files you have on other people in your life?

I invite you to take someone, perhaps that person with whom you are committed to creating a new relationship, and ask yourself:

What is the file—the story—I am living in?

What is holding onto that story costing me?

Am I willing to let go of that story, to shred that file?

If you find you are not, it may be that a deeper forgiveness will need to be summoned.

If the answer to those three questions is yes, replay the evidence in your mind's eye. Replay what happened. Get to the facts. He said this, she said that. Only what is observable.

See if you can account for what happened by looking through a different interpretation structure, one that is more empowering. For example, "all he wants to do is contribute." It might be quite an "a-ha!" moment for you.

Make a commitment to yourself to look through those new eyes the next time you see that person and see what your experience is like.

You will see that the proof of this work's power lives in the *living* of it, not the "knowing." Understanding what I have said will not give you a direct experience of transformation in your relationships. Applying these principles will.

May your work with these principles bring you both insight and joy as you discover that you can disentangle yourself from debilitating stories and adopt new, empowering ones.

I conclude this chapter with the wise words of William Stringfellow:

> *Listening is a rare happening among human beings. You cannot listen to the word another is speaking if you are preoccupied with your appearance or impressing the other, or if you are trying to decide what you are going to say when the other stops talking, or if you are debating about whether the word being spoken is true or relevant or agreeable. Such matters may have their place, but only after listening to the word as the word is being uttered. Listening, in other words, is a primitive act of love, in which a person gives himself to another's word, making himself accessible and vulnerable to that word.*

From *Count It All Joy:*
Reflections on Faith, Doubt, and Temptation Seen Through the
Letter of James

CHAPTER 6

Shifting Your Listening

From Asleep to Awake

If, as Stringfellow says, "Listening is a primitive act of love," the question becomes: how do you get to that "primitive act of love" or "giving yourself to another's word," which is real listening, when you start with a file or with trying to impress the other person?

You may have already noticed, through your experiences of dropping a file, the difference it makes to do so.

Now that you have perhaps had some insight into the kind of listening that connects us to others, or may have begun inventing new ways, new stories, new approaches, or new perspectives as ways to listen to other people in your life, let's take a deep dive into examining listening by putting it under the proverbial microscope. Let's further refine our listening skills.

As Stringfellow suggests in his poem, there are two types of listening that appear in different forms: listening that connects and listening that disconnects; listening that integrates and listening that separates; listening that is vulnerable and listening that is protective. Let us examine both.

Think about a recent conversation you had that did not go well. Why not? Were you bored and then checked out? Where did you go when you checked out?

I call a certain kind of listening, "going to the Bahamas."

I started calling it that after watching a funny video with my husband a long time ago. In it, Steve Martin played an absent-minded waiter. Teri Garr played a patron (a customer) at an upscale restaurant.

Steve, the waiter, asked her for her order and started writing down what she said on his pad. She continued ordering dish after dish after dish. He began to write it all down, writing and writing and writing. Suddenly, he stopped writing and gazed off to his right at the ceiling, with a beatific smile on his face.

Teri Garr, as the customer, looked at him strangely, quizzically, knowing he was somewhere else.

After a long while, he snapped back, suddenly. "Oh," he said, looking at her. "Excuse me. I went to the Bahamas for a moment."

We so often go "off to the Bahamas" with one another, don't we?

Or sometimes, we leave the conversation because we already think we know what they are going to say.

Why bother to stick around when we already know what they are going to say?

Or, sometimes, we already know what they are going to say, so we finish their sentences for them.

Don't you love being interrupted by someone who finishes your sentence? Kills the conversation, doesn't it? And how do you feel when that happens? Honored or shut down?

Or, sometimes they're talking, and their words suddenly trigger a memory of an earlier event in our lives: "Ah, that reminds me of . . ." so we start thinking about that and sometimes speaking about it. In that moment, we interrupt the speaker and shift the conversation away from them. They feel that you don't care about them, or that what they have to say doesn't matter, or that they don't matter. They get triggered themselves. Does this sound familiar?

Or, we are so busy preparing what we're going to say when they finally stop talking that we haven't heard a thing—not a thing, as we are framing our response in our own heads.

Sometimes, they share something with us, and we judge what they say. For example, an internal dialogue might go something like: *That's a really stupid idea.* We may "leak out" our judgment in somewhat polite ways—furrowed brows, a verbal response, rolled eyes, a laugh—yet still, we land a thorn.

Once, I was sharing with someone that we were going to Yosemite Valley the following week. She got a frown on her face. I knew she thought it was a bad idea. She said, "Don't you think it will likely snow that week?"

Or, in another example, someone may share an idea, and we might say, "We tried that just last week, and it just didn't work." Instant deflation.

Or we judge them: *Why does she dress so poorly?* And then we make up a file: *She probably doesn't care what other people think,* or *She's lazy and doesn't respect other people enough to take care of her appearance.*

Another kind of listening is "fix-it." They share a problem they are having, allowing us a glimpse into their world, and we find ourselves immediately focused on *how do I fix their problem?* We jump in to solve it. Or they express some internal state, such as sadness or frustration, and we attempt to "fix" their emotions. They may simply be sharing their experience with us to convey how they feel about something, yet we try to fix it as if it were a problem.

When I share about this particular kind of listening with my participants in my classes, men in the course frequently get wide-eyed, as a sudden insight lands upon them, and say something similar to, "No wonder my wife seems upset with me all the time! I'm always trying to fix her problem or solve her problem, and all she wants to do is share with me!"

In one course, a participant shared with the class on the morning of day two that, after a phone conversation with his wife the night before, the way he paid attention to her and interacted with her completely blew her away. She said, "Ask Amba what she's done with my husband! Why, if that's what you get out of this course, you can stay all week!!!"

That kind of mismatch, where one person only wants to share something from their heart, and the well-intended listener just wants to help "fix it," can be frustrating, separating, and heart-deadening.

Naomi Rachel Remen, a physician and professor of alternative and integrative medicine, wrote an article for the Institute of Noetic Sciences on the difference between fixing, helping, and serving. In it, she writes:

> *Serving is also different from fixing. When I fix a person, I perceive them as broken, and their brokenness requires me to act. When I fix, I do not see the wholeness in the other person or trust the integrity of the life in them. When I serve, I see and trust that wholeness. It is what I am responding to and collaborating with.*

People pick up on how we are relating to them in the background. They hear it, even though the words "you are broken" are never uttered out loud. However, the essence of the relationship, you could say, still gets communicated.

And they feel like you think they are broken, consciously or subconsciously, and resent it. Or, they just feel sad, unworthy, less than, and separated.

Clearly, fixing another is not a good way to sustain a relationship that works—one based on honor, respect, regard, and appreciation for the other—is it?

Here's one important thing to get: all that disconnected listening, what I have just described, *it's all automatic!* You can't help it. You don't want to blame yourself or beat yourself up, because it's simply automatic, triggered, part of the way we are hard-wired. You could call it "animal wiring." We are wired for protection.

So, then, once you see that you are coming from one of these triggered responses, what do you do?

You shift from automatically reacting to *generating* a more powerful listening.

Another way of saying this is that you shift your location from inside your own head, listening to yourself, to being with them.

However, before you can do that, you have to **notice** that you are not *really* listening.

Notice: observe it, see it, catch it, be aware of it.

Awareness is the power that awakens.

Once you are aware, once you have "caught" your reaction, you can choose to *locate* yourself in a place other than your own head.

You intentionally *shift* your location from in here to over there, to them, to where they are.

You be with them. Fully. With nothing going on.

Presence.

Full Attention.

Pure listening.

Wholeheartedness.

Profound honor and respect.

Deep listening.

YOU ARE CONNECTED

When someone is with you wholeheartedly, simply *being there* with you, with pure listening, it's like drinking from a deep well of clear, delicious water when you are thirsty, isn't it?

When someone is with you, simply *being there*, with pure listening, you experience being profoundly known.

When someone is with you, simply *being there*, with pure listening, you know they are interested. You know that they care.

You know that you are loved.

When someone is with you with sacred listening, you begin to come into your own wisdom—wisdom you did not know you had. An intelligence greater than your own brain starts to operate.

You discover answers to questions you have and even questions you did not even know you had.

You have insights. You have *a-has*. You make discoveries.

You are appreciated.

You can move the world.

What are some of the entrances into heart listening that we can start to practice as an art?

When you are committed to connecting with another person, you are curious. You could say, "I am out to discover their world. What's in their world? What are they committed to? Concerned about?"

Because you are interested, because you are out to discover something about them that you did not know before, because you are out to connect with them, you ask questions:

"What did you really mean when you said x?"

Or "Tell me a bit more about what your thinking is behind that thinking."

Or "How come you say that? I don't understand."

Or "I can hear you are passionate about something. Can you tell me more about why you care so deeply about what you are talking about?"

Or "What is the concern that has you say that?"

In other words, you become interested in them. Not like a ploy or a manipulative technique, but because you actually *do* care.

You *are* interested. You *are* curious. You *are* out to discover.

You don't "do" listening in order to have them think you are interested.

Your intention is to *get into their world.*

What is their experience? What's bothering them? What are the commitments and concerns in their world? What are their values? What brings them meaning?

When you listen for discovery, you'll discover! You discover them, you discover the world of their world. Your own world expands, and your capacity to contribute to making a difference with them opens up once you connect with their world.

Listening for the Possibility of Another

When you are committed to empowering others and connecting with them, you listen for the possibility that they are, rather than listening for their limitations.

What keeps us from listening for another as possibility? Our files, our stories, our judgments, and our decisions!

Here's another personal example: when I was teaching high school English, before each semester, we teachers would receive cumulative files on each student. These files listed each student's name and, afterward, what previous teachers thought about that student. I read those once, and I never did it again. You could say it "ruined my listening" for each student. I had to work so much harder just to see them. I was so filled with the stories and views of others that I couldn't see the possibilities in the student right in front of me. I couldn't be with them in real time. I kept listening to someone else's story, someone else's view, someone else's listening.

Sometimes, the previous teacher's comments about a student were positive. I was in trouble there, too. I kept seeing them through a filter of how they should be and what I expected of them based on someone else's experience, and sometimes, they fell short of the ideal pictures in my head. That got me in trouble, as it did not serve them.

Positive files, like negative files, need to be shredded, as well.

Here's an example of the way in which a positive file blocked my access to hearing that a dear friend was making a request.

My friend Naomi was smart, insightful, and loved to explore what lay beneath the surface. She cared deeply about people.

During our years of junior high and high school, we used to have many "sleepovers," during which we talked and talked and talked into the wee hours of the morning. After high school, Naomi became a psychologist. It was a perfect career for her.

One day, maybe twenty years ago, she called me to let me know her father had passed. I knew George; I knew both her parents well. After a long pause, as I took it in and said whatever I could at the time, I asked Naomi if she needed anything from me. She said, "No, I'm fine."

We got off the phone.

About half an hour later, I received another call from her. She said, "When I said I was fine, I was lying. I *want* to talk with you, after all."

We talked for a long time.

After she and I got off the phone, I stopped and questioned myself. I think of myself as being a good listener, as someone who is able to hear what's underneath the words that are being spoken. And yet, I had not heard Naomi's request of me underneath the "no" she spoke when I asked her if she needed anything.

Why not?

Because I had a positive file about her, being a psychotherapist. *She's strong. She knows herself well. She can handle anything. She can take herself through the grieving she needs to do.*

From that time on, I have had my antennae up and out for files, both positive and negative.

Listening for Their Good Intention

That brings us to the next level of depth, the next level of power, and the next opportunity for you to transform yourself and create a connection where none existed before.

For example, initially, the HP manager from the previous chapter believed that his engineer's intention was to waste his time. He was certain of it. He had no doubts about that. As long as he maintained that view, that narrative, and that mindset, the engineer who had been complaining would never have been recognized for his brilliance. He had already been dismissed.

But, as you may recall, the manager caught himself reacting, stopped, apologized to the engineer, and promised to listen. The world changed.

The engineer saw that his boss was, indeed, listening to him, that he was interested in what he had been wanting to say all along. This time, real communication was taking place. The manager was curious. He was *out to discover*. He had hooked into the engineer's intention to make a difference in the business! That means that the manager had a whole, different human being in front of him.

And, what emerged? Brilliance!

Indeed, we might even say that sacred listening is "listening for the brilliance of another."

That inner work of listening to others' brilliance can be magical.

When I thought that my dad's intention was to manipulate me, that's the man I had in front of me. I had to protect myself from that person. When I recognized that his intention and brilliance were to contribute to me, *that* was the man, with his brilliance, who I had in front of me. Someone who was there *for* me, a partner in making my life work.

You can "re-perceive the world and your relationship to it," as Peter Senge says, when he distinguishes what transformational leadership is in *The Fifth Discipline*.

You can dramatically shift your experience of life. You have say-so. You have the power to create. You have the power to choose.

You have the power to choose.

The first step is to become aware. Awareness is the key.

Making This Your Own

I invite you to participate in a playful exercise that may seem challenging and unappealing at first, but it's actually a lot of fun and quite revealing. It also has practical value because, once you practice it as an exercise, you'll be able to recognize when you're being triggered in real life much more quickly. You really get the difference between what a conversation is like when someone isn't listening and the dramatic difference it makes in the quality of the conversation when someone *is* listening.

Here's the experiment you might try on: sit with another person who is willing to do this exercise with you. Share what you have learned from this chapter about the ways people listen.

Both of you think of something you'd love to share with one another: a hobby, a coming vacation, something you love doing, etc.

Pick an "A" and a "B." Now, take turns, one at a time.

A shares what they would love to share, and B "listens" in a way that disconnects, in whatever way they get triggered—judging, going off to the Bahamas, fixing them, or preparing what they are going to say when A stops talking. And speak from those triggered reactions. Feel free to exaggerate those reactions.

Do this for one and a half minutes.

Trade, and B shares while A listens—judging, going off to the Bahamas, fixing them, and preparing what they're going to say next.

Do this for one and a half minutes.

Now, share with each other. How was that for each of you? How did that make you feel?

This exercise will give you a direct experience of how "yucky" it feels to be (not) listened to in this way.

Now, person A shares the same thing again. This time, person B listens for their world. Get interested in their world. Engage with them. Ask questions.

Listen for their brilliance, their wisdom.

Listen for discovery.

Listen for being contributed to.

Trade, and B shares, while A listens from a place of getting interested in their world. Engage with them. Ask questions. Listen for their brilliance. Listen for contributions made by them. Listen for discovery. Be fully attentive and present for them.

Now, address the same questions. How was that for you? What was that conversation like?

Quite different, yes?

Now, I invite you to try this out in real life. Catch yourself when you get triggered. Notice it, and, as soon as you catch it, shift to an empowering listening.

Notice the difference it makes in people's experience when you are fully being with them.

CHAPTER 7

A Parenting Story

From Expectation to Appreciation

I began this book with a welcome on behalf of learning the heart of sacred listening, heart-to-heart listening, with a bow and a greeting: "Tashi Deley."

As I shared, in the high mountains of Tibet, sherpas, pilgrims, monks, and Holy men, all strangers, cross the high, narrow paths, sometimes passing each other. As they pass, they greet each other in a particular kind of way. They bring their palms together in front of their chest, bow slightly, look each other in their eyes, and say, "Tashi Deley."

As an auspicious blessing, it means, "May all good things come to you." Its full meaning is this:

I honor the greatness in you. I honor the place in your heart where lives your courage, wisdom, honor, your intentions, passions, and dreams. I honor the place in you where, if you are at that place in you, and I am at that place in me, there is only one of us.

I am committed to entering my relationships with an inner "Tashi Deley" for every person I meet. I listen for the beauty, courage, and honor in people—their soul, divinity, and the mystery that resides within them.

When you listen to another as God, and you are committed to doing that, God is Who They Are. You can make room for, give space to, however they act. You do not need to buy into their current state of mind or emotion. You can give room to all that external stuff—whether it's anger, frustration, anxiety, or even rage—and listen from your heart to theirs. This isn't easy sometimes, as anger begets anger. Another's anger triggers our own. But if you are committed to connecting, if you are committed to serving, if you are committed to empowering another, if you are committed to relationships that work, you take yourself in hand. You take responsibility for your reactions (they are yours, and nobody else's) by becoming aware of them, and by letting go of your own resistance to the energy that may be coming toward you. You locate yourself over there with them, listening for God.

You'll be amazed at the level of connection you create, even with strangers, when you start to listen that way. People will feel better after just saying hello to you, brighten up, carry themselves a little taller, start conversations easily, and even share their lives with you—a flight attendant, a customer eating at the table near you, a passenger sitting next to you on an airplane, or a waitress. You can even give birth to a new relationship with your son, daughter, wife, husband, or friend by practicing heart-to-heart listening.

As I welcome my participants into my foundational development program, *The Heart of Leadership*, I walk intentionally to the front of the room, offer a welcome from my heart, and share with them how the Tibetans greet each other: "Tashi Deley." Then, I share with them what Tashi Deley means. As I do, I intentionally embody the words that I am saying.

I look each of them in the eye, as I intentionally scan the room, and say,

> *I honor the greatness in you. I honor the place in your heart where lives your courage, wisdom, honor, intentions, passions, and dreams. I honor the place in you where, if you are at that place in you, and I am at that place in me, there is only one of us. Tashi Deley.*

Speaking those words and allowing myself to become one with them sets me straight. It allows me to dive into my own authenticity. And I am there—one with them, each of them.

I am now free to create the course as a conversation with them. They are present with me. Authenticity is the foundation for our conversation.

Who is in that room?

God.

And there, we start the course.

Dacon was in one of my recent courses. She is a highly talented human resources manager at one of the companies I work with. Dressed in khaki pants and a soft peach-colored shirt, with blonde hair, blue eyes, and a medium build, she was attentive, leaning in and listening. I could tell the course was important to her; she wanted a breakthrough.

At the same time, she felt nervous about something. She appeared calm on the outside but was a bit fidgety on the inside, occasionally shifting in her chair throughout the morning session. While she was focused, with her eyes locked onto mine, she would look away now and then, and I could tell she was pondering something meaningful to her.

About two hours into the course, I give each participant the opportunity to share what they are working on in the course, what they want to explore or discover for themselves, or what new possibilities they would like to open up for themselves in the course.

When Dacon came to the front of the room to share with us what she was putting at stake in the course, she said, "I am so worried about my son and my relationship with him. My life has been consumed with trying to connect with him, unsuccessfully, and I've lost my own connection with myself as well. Our relationship just doesn't work, and I don't know what to do about it.

"He has not been doing well in school. He has been diagnosed with ADHD, and sometimes he gets very resistant to his teachers, and he won't listen to me, either. He's a senior now, and his graduation from high school is supposed to be in a couple of months. We don't know if he'll be able to graduate. Sometimes, he even misses his classes, and he won't talk about it. He gets so resistant to me and everyone else. I can't find how to connect with him."

She got more and more real, letting down any guards as she kept speaking. She could see the attention the participants were giving her, the love in their eyes. I could see her on the verge of tears, and she began to cry. Her heart was open, her deeper essence exposed. I could hear her love and care for her son, as well as her concern about herself and her own spirit and life, as this unworkable relationship dominated her well-being.

Throughout the course, Dacon and the other participants continued to explore various approaches to listening to others, with the intention that each person felt known, heard, and understood at the deepest levels of their being. We also investigated different methods of listening to ourselves so that we could remain deeply connected with who *we* are.

We often don't listen. Instead, we pay attention to our own disempowering and frequently judgmental internal chatter. This is what Dacon was doing when she was with her son, Erik.

Later in the course, I had the opportunity to coach Dacon on this relationship.

"When you engage in a conversation with him, what does he say?" I asked her.

"He doesn't really talk to me very much," she replied.

"Do you understand what it's like for him—what his experience is—in his own world?" I inquired.

"No, I really haven't explored that," she said. "I'm mainly scared of him and frustrated that he is so resistant to me. I want to give him advice, but he doesn't want to listen."

I invited this soft-spoken, teary-eyed, loving mother to let go of whatever advice she had for him and to get really, really curious about his world; I mean, not as a technique, but from her heart. To be completely *out* to discover what *his* universe, his world, the world of his fears, his concerns, his disappointments, his anxieties, was like internally for him. To listen without judgment. To listen appreciatively. After all, the only way he would speak was if he felt safe. A deer in the forest leaps quickly away at the first sign of danger. In human interactions, judgment signals danger, even when nothing is spoken aloud. People hear what is unsaid. We can hear another's judgment.

I invited her to let go of her expectations about him. Did she have any? Of course, she did. I invited her to tell us what they were. She gave us a partial list.

We all have our lists of people in our lives with whom we hold expectations. I saw people nodding when I was talking to her, writing things down in their own journals as they had their own insights.

I said to her, "Appreciation means 'to add value to,' and intentionally creating appreciation for another can be an antidote to expectations. All expectations are judgments; 'shoulds' we impose on each other. He should be this way; he should be that way. He should listen to me. He should always go to school. He should always do his homework. He should be a good student."

I told her that her son probably felt judged . . . by everyone—his teachers, his principal, maybe even the other students, and her. The more she could appreciate him and listen to him appreciatively, the greater the chance she had of his opening up to her.

Not only that, but her expectations about him had been constraining her! She said she felt no power around him, that she was out of touch with herself, and that she felt small and controlled by him.

She listened intently. I could tell she was absorbing it. She nodded, releasing many negative thoughts about both herself and him. She recognized that as soon as she could extend grace to herself, to "show up," she could offer him that grace as well. We all felt a profound sense of release. She sat down smiling and at ease.

Later that day, as people were leaving the course until day four, which was scheduled for three weeks later, Dacon said to me, "I'm going to try everything you suggested."

I was thrilled to receive a letter from her between sessions in which she acknowledged, "I realized I had been so consumed with trying to connect with him that I found that I lost *myself* in that search to connect. The weight that was lifted off my heart during the first day we were in class was incredible. Since I've been at home, I've been working very diligently to first reconnect with myself when I am with him and around him. I'm really working on growing a different kind of relationship. It's been a really great experience for me as I navigate this new awareness."

On the morning of day four, everyone shared their experiences over the previous three weeks.

Dacon came confidently to the front of the room and turned around to greet the class. Her smile, which beamed even from her eyes like a ray of sun, communicated her joy before she even began to speak.

She shared with us that her son was overwhelmed by her attention and extremely grateful to her. She mentioned that he opened up to her in ways he had never done before. He began seeking her advice and was receptive to what she said. He followed the advice she offered him regarding actions to take when he missed a day of school. Her guidance proved effective. She felt joyful that she had fostered a new, meaningful relationship with her son, as she hadn't felt connected to him since he was about three years old. She committed to being intentional about her own happiness while strengthening her bond with her son.

I received another letter from Dacon three weeks after the course was over:

> *It's quiet this morning, with the exception of the waterfall from the pool and the sweet sound of birds chirping. I've thought about this program every day since we started in April.*

It's made a profound impact on my life. I was able to give up the power my son had over me. I needed to speak about it out loud to be able to let it go. Your forum provided that opportunity for me to do this. Erik has one more week of school remaining, and we are hopeful his efforts over the last few months have granted him the opportunity to complete high school and graduate. We will know in a week.

Two weeks later, I spoke with Dacon. Erik had graduated from high school with the rest of his class.

I asked Dacon for permission to publish this. In her letter back, not only did she give me permission, but she also said:

"My relationship with Erik continues to blossom. It's really been special. I think he knows how proud I am that he was able to get himself through school. He seems to be maturing.

"I've stepped back from managing his world. I just let him discover and grow. I just show him my love now."

As Andre Auw says, "The gift of heart-listening is, ultimately, the gift of our highest selves, and like all true gifts, one that enriches the giver as much as the receiver."

Making This Your Own

What occurred for you as you read Dacon's story?

Do you have a teenager, or a younger or older child, upon whom you have, either inadvertently or advertently, been laying expectations?

Or, if not your own child, is there someone else—a spouse, a co-worker—with whom you have been harboring expectations?

Ask yourself: what are those expectations?

(You will always have disappointments if you have expectations; the two are like the back and front of the same coin.)

Are you willing to let go of your expectations and see through different eyes?

I suggest the eyes of appreciation.

Appreciation means "to add value to." It can be intentionally cultivated, created, and nourished. Life thrives in the presence of appreciation. Gratefulness is its partner. When appreciation for another is communicated, the relationship deepens.

If so, ask yourself:

What, intentionally, consciously, do you appreciate about your child (or another person)?

Take a moment to imagine them and share with them what you appreciate about them.

Is there something that is there for you to communicate, from your heart to theirs?

What is that? When will you do that?

Is there a question you could ask them that would allow you to get deeper into their world, to understand them, and what they see in a new way?

Take notes or write down any new awareness you have about deepening your relationships with others.

CHAPTER 8

"Honey, You are Just Like Me!"

From Adversary to Soul Sister

Of course, it's not so easy to listen to anyone when you are disturbed, angry, or irritated. It's even harder if they are emotionally triggered, too. It's like you are in a war zone.

I found myself in such a war zone one spring, many years ago, in New York City.

There I was, standing anxiously on a curb, with the horns of New York blaring loudly in the background. The large blue and green doors to the double-decker bus were closed. I wanted in.

It was a very special morning. Five days earlier, we had flown to New York to take my father to Ellis Island. Several years before, I had purchased the rights to inscribe his name, along with my mother's and my stepmother's, on a piece of marble to honor the immigrants who had arrived in this country from elsewhere. Although I had paid for that, neither my father nor I had ever seen the actual monument.

I thought it would be meaningful for him, and for all of us, to see, firsthand, perhaps even touch, his name carved into the marble.

We had saved this outing for the last day of our journey. It was kind of like a pilgrimage, actually. The first step was to get to the southern tip of Manhattan, where we would then take the ferry to Ellis Island.

Of course, there were many modes of transportation—taxis and subways being the obvious choices to reach the southern end. All week long, however, I had envied the people on the upper decks of the buses, mouths agape as they gazed up at the towering buildings stretching into the sky, sometimes disappearing into the fog as the buses crawled through the noisy, traffic-filled streets. I really wanted to experience being on one of those double-decker buses! So did everyone else in my family.

We woke up early that morning to walk to the bus stop. I didn't even stop for coffee because I didn't want to be late. We were so excited! Once we arrived at the ticket office, I approached the counter to purchase our bus tickets. The woman behind the window informed me that each ticket cost twenty dollars. Twenty dollars? For a bus ticket? I was shocked. At that time, it was a significant amount of money. Only later did I discover it included not just a bus ride but a tour as well.

I grudgingly shelled out the money and now found myself standing on the curb: I was on the right, my father in the middle, and Don on his left, waiting impatiently in front of the closed bus door.

We waited for what seemed to be an inordinately long time for those doors to open so we could make a quick beeline to the top floor of the bus.

Finally, the doors opened.

We put our arms through Dad's, helped hoist him up the bus stairs so he would not trip, and started to move quickly to the spiral staircase, winding to the top deck of the bus. I was in the lead.

A large woman stood in front of me, blocking my way. She said to me, and I kid you not, in a loud and angry voice, "Where the *hell* do you think you're going?"

Now, I was already upset, hadn't had my coffee, and was in no mood to be treated so poorly. "*What?*" I said.

She said, "Where the *hell* do you think you're going?"

I swallowed my anger, which was seething inside. Body tight, teeth clenched, I said, as calmly as I could, "I'm going to the top floor of the bus!"

She said, "You're not going *anywhere!*"

It was at this point that I stopped. I knew that if I didn't *stop*, I was about to slam into her, exploding verbally. However, before I did that, I took three or four seconds to visualize a movie in my head, quickly extrapolating into my day, and I realized I was just about to, potentially:

1.   Ruin the rest of the wonderful day we had planned

2.   Ruin the whole trip to New York

So, I came to a stop.

I stopped paying attention to myself and to what my internal voices were saying—like, "How dare she?" "I'm the customer!" "It's her job to take care of me! HOW DARE SHE!"—and shifted my focus. Instead of listening to those internal voices, I placed myself over there with her.

I got into her world.

Was I able to listen for God in her, like we just spoke about? No way!

However, once I connected with her energy, her space, and her world, I realized she was incredibly angry about something.

So, *the best*, the very *best* I could muster was, "You seem angry."

"Angry? You *bet* I'm angry!!!" she said.

"What are you angry about?" I asked.

Still angry, not calm, she said, "He always does this."

"Who always does *what*?" I asked, now genuinely curious.

"He opens the door to the bus," she said.

Now she was calming down. Her voice was quieter. She even noticed I was there and started talking to me like I was a person in her life in front of her.

I said, "Is there something wrong with that?"

"Well, yes," she said, with an unspoken "of course"– not articulated, but resonating clearly in the background.

"What's wrong with that?" I asked, even more curious and interested. Now, we were two human beings, not raging animals, talking to one another.

"He's the bus driver," she said.

"And what's wrong with that?" I asked, my interest and curiosity growing more intense and real by the minute.

And then she spilled it: "Well, I'm the tour guide. *I* should be the one who says when the bus door should open."

Now, I was enlightened about what was inside her world of commitments and concerns.

"Oh!" I said, and then repeated what I just heard, so she understood that I got what she was saying: "So, you feel that because you are the tour guide, *you* should be the one saying when the bus door should open."

"*Yes!*" she said, relieved, eyes wide, lit up, thankful that someone actually understood her. "*I* should be the one," she repeated.

Her whole body relaxed. I could visibly see her muscles loosening.

I said, "OH! I get it." And I did.

I paused, thinking for a second.

"Well," I said, "Have you ever thought about talking with your boss about that?"

"Huh?" she said, looking puzzled.

The idea of that was completely foreign to her. Typically, we don't think about making requests. We often become victims of our circumstances and believe the world is out to get us. We aren't aware that we can actually *influence* the world through speaking and listening. We can make requests. We can create futures that would not come into being unless we had spoken.

"No," she said, wonder in her voice. I could tell she was contemplating the idea of speaking to her boss, and it was clear that she was reflecting on it, despite it being a foreign and strange notion to her.

"Well, you could, you know. You could make a case for being the one who gets to say when the bus door opens, considering your concern for the customer and your awareness of what's happening outside the bus. They might understand your perspective and say 'yes.' On the other hand, they might not and have their reasons for saying 'no.' But you never know. At the very least, you'll have asked."

Her eyes got wide. *Very* wide.

"You know?" she said. "That's a very good idea. I think I'll do that!"

She was now smiling. Broadly. A *big* smile took over her face.

She said, "Okay. You can go on up," gestured for us to go up, and moved her body over so we could pass her, and we climbed the spiral staircase.

About ten minutes later, as we were happily seated on the bench we had selected in the middle of the upper deck, she came by to collect our tickets. I was sitting closest to the aisle, and I gave her the tickets. After I did, she gave me a big smile, leaned in close to my face, looked deep into my eyes, patted my knee, and said in a big, booming voice, "Honey? You are *just like me!*"

We had seen into each other's hearts, and we recognized the divine in each other.

She had experienced that we were one.

CHAPTER 9

It Was All in the Stopping

Awakening Awareness

Between stimulus and response, there is a space.
In that space lies our freedom and our power to choose our response.
In our response lies our growth and our happiness.
Anonymous

That day in New York was a great teaching moment for me.

Let's examine that incident under the microscope and see what secrets we can uncover and what keys we can find to gain ever more open access to the heart of deep listening.

There was indeed a key—a key that appeared in a singular moment—that allowed me to "save the day" and shift from disconnection to connection with our guide. Do you see what that moment was?

It was stopping. When I paused and realized I was highly agitated and about to verbally lash out at our guide, stopping marked the very beginning of "saving the day." By noticing my reaction, I became awake. I became aware. I recognized that I was in a triggered response.

You might think this is not a big deal. I suggest that you consider it a big deal. That moment of noticing is everything.

Next, in about three seconds, I envisioned in my mind's eye what the future would look like if I chose that disastrous path. I realized the effect my reaction could have on the entire celebratory day I had planned.

It was way more important to me to have a great day with Dad and Don than to be right about being mistreated or not taken care of as the customer.

And, as I said in the story, while initially "listening for God" in that woman was nowhere within my capacity to create, I could, at the very least, "get into her world."

At that moment, I transformed internally from listening to my own screaming internal voices—feeling affronted and thinking about the unfairness of it all—to truly being present with her. When I was *with* her, I noticed that she was angry. I could easily express to her, with concern, "You seem angry."

Those three simple words sparked a new dialogue—a genuine conversation, a conversation in which "real" communication could now take place.

It is in noticing, catching, and releasing whatever has been triggered that miscommunication ends and communication begins. Listening, with a small "I," ceases, and Listening, with a big "*L*," true Listening, starts.

You could call it "catch, release, and shift." It's easy to remember, but not so easy to practice, especially when your reactions have overtaken you.

That's the work. It takes discipline, vigilance, alertness, and a commitment to being awake—a commitment to not leading a life of suffering; a commitment to making life work.

Making This Your Own

I invite you to pause the next time you become aware that you are feeling fear, irritation, anger, bewilderment, or confusion. Take a moment to consider the effect or consequence of expressing your reactions out loud and laying them on someone.

See if that creates space for you to simply notice your reactions, allow them, keep them to yourself, own them, and let them go.

But what do I do with my triggered reactions, you might ask?

Ah, that's our very next chapter . . .

CHAPTER 10

What Do I Do with My Triggered Reactions?

Catch, Release, and Shift

In a previous chapter, I said, "You must be more interested in being happy than in suffering."

"Of course, I am!" you say.

Yet, many of us spend our whole lives suffering, unaware that we have unknowingly become one with our negative thought patterns. We live our whole lives in that ignorance.

Here's an old story:

> *A grandfather is telling his grandson about a fight that is going on inside himself.*
>
> *He said it is between two wolves.*
>
> *One is evil: anger, envy, sorrow, regret, fearful thinking, greed, arrogance, self-pity, guilt, resentment, inferiority, lies, false pride, superiority, and ego.*
>
> *The other is good: joy, peace, love, hope, serenity, humility, kindness, benevolence, empathy, generosity, truth, compassion, and faith.*
>
> *The grandson thought about it for a minute, and then asked his grandfather, "Which wolf wins?"*
>
> *The grandfather simply replied, "The one I feed."*

"The one I feed."

Which wolf are you feeding in any given moment?

Having the awareness of which wolf you are feeding enables you to shift the universe you inhabit. If you are old enough, or Sci-Fi oriented enough, you will remember the "wormholes" in *Star Trek*, where the great star cruiser, The Enterprise, would be transported from one section of the galaxy to another by being sucked through a "wormhole."

When you are *aware*, you are living in a state of Pure Presence. You can let your reactions simply *be*. Your reactions, then, will let *you* be. You could say awareness is a key to freedom.

Know that you are human—perfectly imperfect—and that the reactive mind is part of the package. Therefore, you don't have to blame or criticize yourself when you find yourself caught up in your reactions. Allow yourself the grace of being human. Forgive yourself. Extend grace to yourself. And once you notice, you can set yourself free.

The mind that operates in survival mode triggers its reactions automatically, in almost no time! When someone says or does something you don't like, you react immediately. Then, you express that reaction (anger, fear, blame, etc.) when speaking to them. In turn, they respond to *your* reactions. That's how human drama unfolds. It's a rapid downward spiral toward chronic miscommunication. The other person is perceived as a threat, leading both individuals to close off and feel the need to protect themselves.

However, if you can catch those reactions, notice them, recognize them, and name them, rather than becoming identified with them, if you can experience them and accept them rather than *press* against them or resist them, you will find yourself in another world.

I invite you to apply what I suggest to your life, experiment with it, play with it, and see what opens up when you do.

When we *are* our positions, our beliefs, and our files, the proverbial finger is pointed squarely in the direction of the other person. "It's their fault."

We blame them, and we are the victim—a self-satisfying feeling to be sure, as it allows us to be "off the hook."

But when we embrace the declaration, "Only I am responsible for my reactions," and stop blaming, shaming, and guilt-tripping, and instead choose to take *responsibility for everything*, everything shifts. You find freedom.

Freedom and responsibility go together.

So, what do you do with your reactions?

You accept them. You let them be. You notice.

But first, you must be aware that your reactions are running the show and catch them as they arise.

Here are some ways to relate to your reactions so that they don't run the show.

Remember when you were a child and would lie on your back on the grass in your backyard, perhaps with a friend, playfully imagining and identifying what the shapes of the clouds looked like?

"Look!" you'd say to your friend, "There's a lion! Oh, look, he's changing into a great blue heron! And now, it's a newborn baby! . . . Oh wow!!"

But do we still do that? No!

No. We have a reaction that has somehow, suddenly been triggered quite automatically, and we don't let it pass us by like clouds in the sky. We say, looking at the cumulus cloud of anger, "Anger? Let me grab hold of you!" And we pull it in and hold it tight to our chest or put it on like a vest. We become it.

"Fear? Okay, I am yours!" And we become smaller than our fear, which swallows us up like a great, ugly, dark behemoth from the deep.

"There's an 'I'm not worthy' cloud! Let me dance with you for the rest of my life!"

Rather than let them go by, like clouds in the sky, we identify with those reactions.

If, on the other hand, we notice these reactions, allow them, accept them, recognize them, and observe them, something extraordinary happens. We are free! We disidentify from our minds.

We are *free*!

You'll have to practice this, like you do with any discipline, to have a direct experience of what I am talking about. It takes practice and discipline to recognize your reactions.

Note: I use these words interchangeably: accept, recognize, notice, catch, become aware of, and be mindful—they all essentially mean the same thing.

Awareness opens up a new space: the space of choice, the space for *creating* listening in a different way or for one another. We can choose to truly be with them, to be present to them, to immerse ourselves in the world of their concerns, just as I did with the Manhattan double-decker bus tour guide, or Dacon did with her son, or I did with my father when I was younger. Empathy starts to show up. Compassion shows up. Love shows up.

But first, we have to deal with "the drunken monkey." Buddha described the human being as being filled with drunken monkeys. What a great image! You can visualize it: monkeys jumping around, screeching loudly in the jungle, screaming at us that we're not good enough, howling about everything that can go wrong, constantly sounding alarms, distracting us with their chatter. The "monkey mind" keeps us from fulfilling our passions, accessing our creativity, and connecting with one another. It keeps us from just plain being present and being here now. And, of course, it keeps us from empowering others.

Therefore, mindful awareness practice is critical. When you commit to being fully present, you can treat all of life as a form of meditation.

When you have mindful awareness of your reactions, you can simply embrace them and "invite them in," as the thirteenth-century mystic Rumi says in his well-known poem "This Being Human Is a Guest House." Once invited in, the resistance stops, and we are calm. We have the opportunity to be our authentic selves.

I have found his words so meaningful, I am sharing with you his entire poem:

This being human is a guest house.
Every morning a new arrival.
A joy, a depression, a meanness,
some momentary awareness comes
as an unexpected visitor.
Welcome and entertain them all!
Even if they're a crowd of sorrows,
who violently sweep your house
empty of its furniture,
still, treat each guest honorably.
He may be clearing you out
for some new delight.
The dark thought, the shame, the malice,
meet them at the door laughing,
and invite them in.
Be grateful for whoever comes,
because each has been sent
as a guide from beyond.

I love that: "Each has been sent as a guide from beyond."

What if we could look at everything and everyone we encounter as a "guide from beyond?"

Making This Your Own

Before moving on, I invite you to take a moment to pause and consider writing down or journaling the insights you've gained about your life, as well as any practices you'd like to adopt to begin integrating "catch, release, and shift" into your life.

You might even keep a daily journal of times you've "lost it" and then caught and released, reconnecting with yourself, with another, and with your own heart.

CHAPTER 11

Building Relationships

The Foundation for Everything

By this time, you might be thinking, *Wow, this is hard! It takes practice, attention, vigilance, and discipline. Do I even have to bother?*

Here's a simple truth: Relationships, partnerships, and collaboration can make what seems impossible possible.

Relationships can turn a "no" into a "yes."

Here's a very personal story, a story of my husband's and my life, where we get to live, and the life we are blessed to lead. This life would never have come to pass had it not been for a relationship we developed with the people who were possibly to become our next-door neighbors; two of the most incredibly gracious people I have ever known.

The year was 1989. We decided to leave our woodsy home in the Bay Area and move *somewhere* where we could live on the water year-round *if* we could afford it. (It was a big if.) We began our search.

We were committed to buying waterfront property. Here's the backstory:

Don's childhood summers were spent on a pristine, yet lesser-known, fifty-mile-long island, now known as Isle Royale National Park. Don's great-grandfather bought the land, and his grandmother built a cabin there with the help of a neighbor fisherman. Don and his parents, brothers, and cousins went there every summer. Don and I still go there almost every summer, living like the "old timers" lived in the thirties, pumping lake water (now filtered, of course) out of the lake; trudging down a well-worn, sometimes moose-turd-laden path to the outhouse, known as the "biffy" (sometimes in the middle of the night); cooking with propane; lighting the cabin with kerosene lamps; and bringing in plenty of ice. There are no cars on the island, and the Gale cabin is off the grid.

In the island's quiet, Nature reveals her teachings through the call of the loon, the lapping of the waves on the rocks, the gentle, tiny purple wildflowers that emerge from the lava rock, and the turbulent storms.

What particularly attracts me is being present with the water all the time, observing and being at one with the lake like a never-ending moving sculpture, and dancing with the wind, mirroring the sun and the moon. I love the sun's reflection on the water and receiving the lessons of impermanence that the flux of nature can bring us if we quiet down enough.

One summer in the late eighties, we both realized, "Hey! Maybe we could live on water year-round!" We both loved the idea.

So, we started searching. We began with the Bay Area, where we were already living. However, we found it to be so unaffordable that our search in that location ended in only two days.

Meanwhile, I had been leading communication courses in Seattle and was inspired, and perhaps even awestruck, by the beauty of the Northwest—the trees, the water, the mountains . . . it felt like a separate haven on the planet, resplendent with glory.

We began exploring this region of the world. We traveled to Canada, drove around Vancouver Island with a friend, and discovered that it was beautiful and feasible. We both realized, however, that we did not want to move out of the U.S. after all. Our next stop was Northern Washington, and while we continued searching for affordable waterfront properties, nothing seemed to "fit."

Approximately a year into the search, in 1989, we were introduced to a real estate agent who, in turn, invited us to look at a piece of land for sale on an island named Bainbridge, across from Seattle. We loved the feel of Bainbridge. Farms, a thick second-growth forest that you can meander through, houses that resemble Cape Cod homes, and a large and friendly family-owned grocery store that sells organic produce and grass-fed beef, which my friend, Ruth, calls "the spiritual center of Bainbridge Island." There were no high-rises, and lots of creative, active people, committed people who were out to make a difference. I remember the first time we crossed Puget Sound on the ferry, standing at the front of the boat, wind whistling across my face, hearing the gulls, and smelling the sea. On that first ferry ride across the Sound, a great sense of being at peace almost overwhelmed me. Imagine living on an island where the primary mode of transportation to the mainland was by boat! (Just like Isle Royale!)

The land we were shown was on the water and within our price range on this extraordinary island. That was amazing! However, we discovered that there was a reason it was within our price range. It was a steep, steep piece of land on the water, almost impossible to build on. We were told it had been on the market for eight months before we saw it, with the proverbial "no bites."

A scattered forest of alder, fir, and cedar populated the steep slope down to the shore.

We loved it. The neighbors were welcoming, interesting, and so enjoyable to be with. We needed to determine if building here was feasible. We set out to perform our due diligence, maintaining a mindset of "No matter what, we are going to go to the ends of the Earth to see if it's possible to purchase this property."

We remained committed and intentional.

Could we install a curtain drain to handle the Northwest rains? Could we build a proper bulkhead to keep the land from sliding into the sea? Where would the house go? Where would the sewer system go? Where would the well house go?

During the entire vetting process, we were warmly welcomed to this pristine, beautiful, and timeless place by Wayne and Anne Blair, who would be our next-door neighbors if we were able to build. They lived in a lovely home aptly named "Cedar Hall," next door to what could be "our property." Even though the land adjacent to them had been vacant throughout their years of living there, they welcomed us with warm smiles, generosity, hospitality, and kindness of heart.

They invited us into their home and treated us to dinners on their front porch or in their cozy dining room. We met their children and shared warm, enjoyable moments together, discussing our visions, our work in the world, what is meaningful to us, our concerns, and what we care about. We liked each other very much and appreciated each other's company.

As the exploration process continued and we received answers to our questions, it began to look like building there might actually be feasible, and we began. We found a dedicated, artistic architect and an all-in, independent contractor.

As the process moved forward, I became attached, longing to be able to make the move to this particular piece of land feasible and to be able to "close the deal."

And then, about six months into the vetting process, we were stopped cold.

We discovered that there was no place to dig a well. While I knew nothing about building, I learned that a well had to be placed a certain distance away from the septic system. Because of the peculiar triangle of the property lines, we couldn't fit both the septic system and the well within that space.

We felt confused, upset, sad, and disappointed.

We sat stunned by the disappointing news about the well. Our hearts were broken, as we had ultimately become attached to the idea of moving there.

We sat with it, reflected on it, worked with it, and accepted it, all while not giving up on the idea. We acknowledged our disappointment, sadness, and even despair as we continued to hold space for the possibility of something to appear that could not be seen right now.

And it did.

Don and I took a pilgrimage to Esalen in Big Sur, where we had each spent much time individually before we met, as we each dove into our own spiritual development in our twenties. Esalen, you may remember, is that special place on the Big Sur coast, where, in 1972, I was first opened to a new world of higher frequencies, energy, and Spirit. Returning there now was wonderful. Don and I relaxed. Deeply. We breathed in the salt air as we took long walks, listening to the wild waves crashing on the boulders beneath the baths. We let go of the stressful, negative conversations that had been eating away at our peace of mind and allowed ourselves to tap into an intuitive wisdom way larger than our left brains.

One evening, an idea struck both of us like a bolt of lightning from heaven. "Hey!" I said to Don. "Remember? Wayne has been complaining about his water."

To which he responded, "Yes!" And then, completing my own thought, he said, "I have an idea! Let's make them an offer that they won't want to refuse. Let's offer to build a Class IV well on their property, which we could all share."

When we came back to Bainbridge, Don made the offer.

They loved the idea of it. The impossible had been made possible.

We've all been enjoying that pure, clear water for many years.

We could finally respond with a "Yes!" to our anxious real estate agent, who wanted us to proceed much more quickly than we were. Now, the sale could finally close.

Were it not for that nurturing relationship and sense of partnership, we would never have had our home where we do, on the water, surrounded by the tall firs, cottonwood, and cedar trees.

That relationship made our new home on this beautiful island in the Pacific Northwest possible, and we are infinitely grateful.

And now, if you come to visit us, you will see the well house on their property.

The Blairs were given to our hearts as a gift.

Here is a related thought:

When we built our home, our architect, contractor, and we spent considerable time, energy, and thought designing and laying the foundation. Our first primary focus was on building that foundation.

When you want to accomplish anything that involves other people, the same principle applies. The larger the project, the more time, energy, and intention need to be invested in laying the foundation of a relationship among all participating members. The size and strength of the relational foundation you are building need to match the size of the accomplishment you are committed to fulfilling.

If you want to buy a ticket for the movie theater, that's simple—you might smile and exchange small talk with the vendor. If you want to have a fine dining experience, you might want to go out of your way a bit to establish a relationship with your server, as that relationship will be an integral part of your experience. If you want to generate a considerable accomplishment as a team, you will want to exercise the muscle of sacred listening. You will want to spend the time and initiative to create and sustain relationships that work.

The keyword in that last sentence is "sustaining." Just as relationships can be built, they can be broken.

When they are broken, they must be healed. Otherwise, everything stops, like what happened with Doug, whose story I will share with you in the next chapter.

Doug's heart had grown hard and brittle, and then transformed, growing soft and loving through the gift of Deep Listening.

Making This Your Own

Here are some questions you might reflect upon:

Who are the people in your life who have been gifts to your heart?

Who are the people or relationships in your life who, were it not for them, your own vision or dream for a future would not have been fulfilled?

Is there a relationship in which you would like to express your appreciation? If so, when will you do so?

How will you do so?

Call them?

Write them a handwritten letter?

Send them a card?

Invite them out for lunch?

Where in your life, given what you are up to, is it time to build stronger relationships?

When is it time for you to focus on strengthening the weak foundation of a relationship?

CHAPTER 12

Listening Heals

Creating a Safe Space

*With the gift of listening comes the gift of healing,
because listening to your brother or your sister until they have said
the last words in their hearts is healing and consoling. Someone has
said that it is possible to 'listen a person's soul into existence.'*
Catherine Doherty
Author and contemplative

I met Doug in 1979, when I was an enrollment manager in Phoenix. Lloyd Fickett, the center manager, had invited me to join the staff of the newly opened center. I was thirty-four years old.

Doug was on a team with about forty other graduates of the *est* training I mentioned at the beginning of my book. They were all volunteers, eager to share their experiences with others considering attending that workshop themselves.

That small band of volunteers and I had a lot of fun. We loved sharing what had opened for us personally, we loved the opportunity to serve, we loved the people we were serving, whether or not they decided to participate in the program, and we loved one another. We were tight. We worked as a team. We communicated, and we appreciated one another.

For about a year, everything was great. Our statistics were through the roof. The program was new to the Phoenix area, and the graduates were eager to invite their friends to this opportunity.

About a year into the program, everything took a downturn. I didn't know why.

Doug was one of the volunteers with whom I shared an extraordinarily positive relationship. He was a cheerful young man of about twenty-eight, with brown-red hair, a slender build, and an easy-to-be-around demeanor, accompanied by a gentle, bright smile. Doug was also consistently one of the top producers on the team. At one point, over a couple of weeks, Doug's results began to decline. At first, I gave it space and didn't say anything; everyone experiences downtime. I dismissed it, assuming he'd pick everything back up on his own once he sorted things out.

After about a week or two with no results, I asked Doug, "Hey! How's it going? I noticed your results are down. Is everything all right?"

I was in a hurry when I made that statement. In other words, my heart, my presence, wasn't in that question. I didn't really care. I just wanted him to start producing. I was concerned. He said, "Yep, everything is fine."

He was as shallow as I was, though I was not aware of it. I mean, I was busy. I had a lot to do. I didn't slow down enough to really listen. I later discovered that he "knew" I was not really present for him in those moments.

About a week later, with results continuing to plummet, I stopped Doug on his way out of the office that day and asked, "What's happening?"

He looked at me, glanced down, and replied, "Nothing."

I urged, "What's going on? Your results are down."

Still staring at the floor, he replied, "It's okay. Don't worry about it."

I said, "Okay. Glad to hear. Get your results up, would you?"

Does this sort of exchange sound at all familiar to you?

Around that time, my manager, Lloyd—a dark-haired man in his mid-thirties with a warm smile that emanated kindness, an angular yet gentle face, and a small goatee—called me into his spacious office. He shut the door.

"Have you noticed Doug's results have gone down the tubes?" he asked.

I said, "Of course I have."

He said, "What are you going to do about it, or what have you done?"

I told Lloyd I've talked with him a few times every other day, to no avail.

He stopped. He looked at me. He looked at me intentionally. He said, "Amba. Have you ever considered that Doug may be withholding something from you? That he might be in fear of telling you what's really going on with him? That you might not be a safe space for him? In fact, you might be feeling like a threat to him?"

Lloyd's words stopped me. Although Lloyd spoke lovingly and softly, it felt as if a loud cymbal clang shook my heart and awakened me.

Of course!

I had written him off. I had not truly been there for him. Because I had "position power," it made sense that he might view me as a threat, especially since I had stopped seeing and listening to him as a valuable human being with his own life and feelings. I had asked him superficial questions—questions that held no heart, no authenticity, no curiosity, no search for discovery, and no caring. I had closed my heart to him, and he had closed his heart to me. He wasn't about to speak his truth in a space that felt so profoundly unsafe.

As I opened the door to Lloyd's office to leave, he stopped me again, this time saying, "Amba." I turned around. He said pointedly, "Let this conversation transform who you are as a manager."

I thought to myself, *Whoa! I have work to do.*

I did . . . let it transform me.

The first action I took was to call Doug and authentically apologize. I intended to carve out a space for a conversation that was deep, vulnerable, real, had plenty of spacious time, and could make a difference in restoring a lost relationship.

I let him know I was aware I hadn't really been listening, nor had I created an opening for him to truly communicate what was in his heart. I promised to be a safe space for him, a space of no judgment, no criticism, only listening for what he had to say to me, and particularly what he had not been saying, anything he might be in fear of speaking. I promised him I would be open to really hearing him, even if it was hard.

We set up a time for a meeting in a room where we would not be interrupted, and with no end time, no "stuff to do" afterward. As we began our meeting, I told him that if what he had to say triggered an automatic reaction that made me defensive, I promised to catch, release, and shift so that I could be fully present and listen to his concerns and unexpressed feelings. I also asked him to let me know at any time if he felt I wasn't fully hearing him, and we would start over with that communication until he "got" that I had received, fully received, without resistance, what he had to say.

The conversation lasted about three hours. He asked me to listen to something more than once. During that conversation, I had many revelations. I realized how callous and superficial my actions had been. In my push for results, my need to hurry, and my fear that we wouldn't achieve outcomes, I had stopped caring about the volunteers and their big, generous hearts. I had also stopped caring about the people we served. They all became numbers.

While I don't remember his exact words, I can share with you the essence of what he said that evening.

He told me how excited he had been to share an experience that made such a difference in his own life with others, even strangers, who might then engage with it for themselves.

He shared how much he loved being a part of a team, a family, really, of volunteers who were serving people and whose lives were dedicated to a commitment larger than themselves.

He told me how much he appreciated my enthusiasm and how he had been learning so much from me about the art of enrollment, serving others, and creating opportunities for others to take action and inspire their lives.

He told me he had been having so much fun.

He told me how much he relied on me to "live the work"—to be gracious, even under pressure, and to serve as a mentor by being a model.

Then he shared a specific story with me, a story about how, one night, I had deeply disappointed him.

We were debriefing with the team after an introductory seminar, sitting in a circle and reflecting on what had worked and what had not. He said, "It was painfully obvious to me, and to everyone, that you were disappointed in me and my results that night. The way you communicated that was humiliating. I was embarrassed in front of the group. I didn't want to say anything to you, especially in front of the group, and you didn't stick around long enough for me to have a private word with you, though I'm not sure I would have then. I felt too embarrassed and ashamed."

He had gone home that night disheartened.

He didn't want to play anymore.

And, not wanting to say anything about it even the next day, because I was, after all, "the boss," he had kept his mouth shut.

He shared with me that, at the next event, he entered the room feeling disheartened, dispirited, and disappointed in himself, fearing he would once again let me down.

He remembered that I had told him to "get his energy up," which had the opposite effect.

He continued to come to the center to work, make calls, and participate in guest seminars, not out of passion or commitment from his heart—two essential ingredients for that kind of work—but because he had made an agreement with the center.

And the results matched.

I didn't know what to do. I was disappointed, not acknowledging, not even *recognizing*, my own disappointment, my own anger, and my own fear beneath the surface. I blamed him. I had made commandments to him that didn't work, like, "Hey! Get your results up, would you?"

He told me that he felt like he had lost both a friend and a coach. He felt that he had lost a life that was enjoyable and life-giving. Instead, it felt draining and painful.

His body kept attending events, but his heart and spirit were not there.

As he continued to share all this with me, the space continued to feel increasingly safe for him. He spoke honestly. I listened deeply to get layers under the surface, with compassion and empathy, for him and for myself.

The bottom line is, he had felt betrayed by me. Having felt betrayed myself a few times in my life, I know how heartbreaking it is, and that one wants to develop a "brittle" heart, with walls around it, to protect oneself.

You can't enroll people in saying "Yes!" to a life-altering, life-transforming, life-inspiring conversation when their heart is brittle.

As the conversation progressed, I became increasingly moved, and our hearts softened.

As my heart awakened, so did Doug's. As Doug's heart opened, so did mine. At the end of the evening, what was present was love, connection, and sacred listening.

In the end, I asked him with my whole heart to forgive me, and he did.

We hugged. We cried. We experienced being at one with each other in this sacred heart space.

A few days later, Doug was in a seminar for guests, fully present. He was such a safe and loving energy that three people enrolled in the program that night in a small gathering with him.

Later, I realized that I must have behaved similarly with the others. I held individual meetings with each team member to "listen with the ear of my heart."

I am so grateful for the gift Doug gave me. The love and caring honesty he shared with me shifted me—it shifted who I was as a manager, just as

Lloyd had asked. But more importantly, it shifted who I am as a person, a listener, and a being.

Making This Your Own

Bring to mind the last time you listened to another in this deep manner. What was that like for you? And for them?

Bring to mind the last time another truly heard you, and you spoke your heart, and love became present.

Experience the feeling of that soft tenderness.

Who in your life could you listen to in that way, or who is calling to you to listen from your heart?

Who could you ask to listen to you in that way, who may be reticent to do so? In what ways might you open new territory for them to listen in that way?

CHAPTER 13

Being a Great Leader

Courage, Humility, Commitment

Fifteen engineers, all male, between the ages of thirty and sixty, sat around a rectangular table with their manager. They all looked down at the table and occasionally looked up at me as I was speaking. They were clearly angry, many of them red-faced, some squirming in their seats, unwilling to communicate, reticent, and skeptical about the meeting that had been called—a meeting on behalf of cleaning up the past and creating a new beginning for the division.

A week earlier, Dale had called me on the phone, declaring an emergency.

Dale was the senior manager of the facilities department of Hewlett Packard's Corvallis Site, and he and his team had been asked, three months before his call to me, to build a new manufacturing facility for the division.

There was a problem. None of his team wanted to work or to communicate what was going on with them. All work had stopped.

The project of building the new fabrication facility was stalled.

Dale was frustrated, upset, and, as they say, "beside himself."

Interesting expression, that. Not really himself, but beside himself. Frankly, he was lost. He didn't know what to do.

Just as we saw in Doug's story, when things don't work, when everything stops, and nothing moves forward, it is almost always the case that honest communication, too, has stopped; that no real speaking or listening has occurred.

People are afraid to speak because they are afraid of not being heard; they are afraid that there is no one, absolutely no one, who will lend a listening ear from an open, awakened heart. They were fearful that if they did speak, they would be fired.

On that first call, Dale told me his guys had simply stopped working. He did not know why. However, he was suspicious. And wise. He thought maybe, just maybe, there was some incompletion from the past, and through my coming to facilitate this critical discussion for a day, we could help get them moving again.

He had done enough work with me, work that had been supported over the years by the senior leadership, to know how pervasive an incomplete past can be. It can color the present, render what seems to be doable as undoable, and keep any forward-moving progress from happening.

He was right.

Before we met with the team, I coached Dale by himself. Dale was open to being coached and hungry for it. He wanted, more than anything, for things to start moving again. You could say he was "at stake."

Effective coaching can take place when people have a lot at stake. When they are casual or don't care very much, it cannot. John Wooden would never have taken on coaching a player who might play basketball "someday."

That day, I told Dale that whatever had gone on in the past was probably going to be difficult—and, at first, seemingly impossible—for them to communicate about. I told him that people were probably still angry about something (we didn't know what) that had occurred in the past, and that the conversation might become difficult to hear.

The anger, disappointment, and fear—whatever had been triggered—had also been buried, never spoken aloud. Therefore, for this conversation to work, he had to let go of any attachment to a particular position he held. A position is like a belief or a point of view through which one sees the world. His own staff probably had a different perspective, or "position," and he needed to be open to hearing it, whatever it was.

So, he would need to notice if he got defensive. He would need to keep his awareness antennae up for any sign of his mind kicking in with *but, but, but* or wanting to defend himself or his position in any way. Our ego gets involved in conversations like this. We think, of course, that we are right.

I told him I would be a support to him in that, and if he did close down or get defensive, I wanted his permission to let him know in front of the group that that had happened. He gave it to me readily.

Dale was ready for a breakthrough. He was also open, courageous, generous, and committed to supporting the team so they could begin to work well again.

We talked about what he would say to create a safe space for each person on his team to speak freely. In this space, there would be no repercussions, no judgments held on to for the future, and no grudges—just pure, deep listening. I didn't call it "sacred listening" at the time, but that is what I meant by it.

That had to be more important to him than being right about anything that had happened in the past.

We met in a generic, beige-colored meeting room for a day, starting at 8:00 a.m. and ending around 8:00 p.m. on the same day. The room had no plants or colors, just bare walls and a rectangular table with seventeen chairs. It was filled with sixteen very unhappy people.

It took two hours to set the stage. I let them know Dale had called me and why we were there. They had already worked with me, knew me, and trusted me. I promised a safe space, and so did Dale.

I handed it over to Dale. Dale announced the purpose of the meeting: to create an environment in which communication could take place that would free everyone up to communicate on behalf of restoring their passion for their work. He told them he appreciated what capable engineers they were—guys who loved the company, their division, and loved their jobs. He told them that the purpose was to create a space of communication in which whatever had not been said could be said, understood, and received, and open up the possibility for work to begin anew on creating the new facility.

He said, "I called Amba because I am more committed to restoring a good environment in the workplace for us again than just about anything. I think the work has stopped because you haven't felt I would hear you or listen to you, and that maybe, even, you might lose your job if you spoke up. I promise no repercussions from today." He expressed that he was committed to experiencing, with compassion, each person's reality.

He promised that if he became defensive or reactive, he would let them know and listen to what they were saying again. If anyone felt that they had not received or gotten what they expected, they could say so. The conditions had to be safe. Everyone had to feel free to speak. After two hours of setting the stage, the guys were still skeptical but more open than they had been when they first came into the room.

The first brave person gingerly began to "test the waters" to see if Dale meant what he said.

Leaning in with his body, as if his life depended on getting the first engineer's point of view, Dale was totally present, with nothing else going on. He received everything the first engineer shared with him. I invited him to share his experience honestly with Dale, to express what had happened that had hurt him.

At first, he said he had been thrilled to have been hired by Dale. He regarded Dale like a father and counted on him to make the right decisions. He had poured his life into his work. When it was time to build a new manufacturing facility fifteen years before, they all "put their backs into it," embracing the opportunity to work at 100 percent.

And then, about three months into the project, Dale decided to outsource it on his own. He never consulted his team. The first engineer who was speaking shared how deeply he had felt betrayed and let down by Dale's solo decision, like he didn't matter, his feelings didn't matter, what he thought didn't matter, and his participation didn't matter.

He felt like a mechanical cog in a mechanical wheel, not like he was being cared for or that his opinion was being respected. When Dale "dismissed him"—or at least that is how it felt to him—he was radically hurt.

He spoke for about forty-five minutes. Dale stayed present the whole time. Tears were in his eyes. Dale had gotten it and received it.

There was a pause, and we all took a deep breath, letting ourselves sit in the silence that followed.

After a pause, I asked this first brave gentleman if he would be willing to forgive Dale.

He looked at him. Somehow, in that space of open and honest communication, forgiveness had already occurred. The resentment that had been festering for years had already been released through this simple communication process.

And, fully completing the conversation, with tears in his eyes, he said to Dale, "I forgive you."

When forgiveness awakens, the heart opens. Tears followed, and both men allowed themselves to hug one another; to be moved by their love for one another. The relationship was restored.

We will explore forgiveness in a future chapter. Here, I'd like to point out that forgiveness is the key to completion; this first man's willingness and generosity of heart became a turning point not only for himself but also for others in the group. They saw that Dale truly meant it when he promised to listen, reconnect with each person, and create a safe space for a new beginning.

A new peace came into being, and a new future was born.

One by one, each engineer at the table shared their experiences, stories, decisions, conclusions, thoughts, and feelings, until everything was spoken and received. A few times, someone requested a repetition, and at times, I intervened, but mostly, they managed it themselves.

With each person speaking and being real, the truth of each person's experience was communicated and received. People shared their experiences honestly and forthrightly, and Dale got it all.

Each person was generous and open, and willing to forgive.

A healing took place, and a sense of wholeness returned.

They found themselves in new territory, the territory for a new beginning.

Like all the speakers, Dale was courageous, generous, and open. His profound commitment to honesty and real communication—listening from the heart—carried the day.

When we returned from our afternoon break at around 3:00 p.m., I asked if anyone had a request. Sometimes, new beginnings begin with a new commitment. The engineers looked at each other and asked to talk alone, so Dale and I left the room.

We returned to the room when someone called us back in. One person crystallized it: "Since the market conditions are the same, we request that if it occurs to you at any time during this project of building this new fab that you even consider outsourcing, you stop, you do nothing. You call a meeting. And we, together, look at the facts together in a conversation and decide collectively whether to outsource."

"Are you willing to accept our request?"

Dale said emphatically, "Yes."

Now, the *team*work could begin.

It just so happened that their request was indeed fulfilled about eight months later. Dale called his team together. Together, they chose to outsource.

And together, with the project being completed through later outsourcing, the facility was built.

The team had emerged as one coordinated body, respectful of one another, a foundation of communication and integrity upon which they stood.

For the next twenty years, such conversations, which centered on aligning through communication, inventing new possibilities, rendering them feasible, and creating coordinated action, remained at the heart of the extraordinary success of their inkjet business.

The visionary leaders of the inkjet business remained deeply committed to spiritual principles and communication practices, as we've just witnessed, woven into the fabric of the culture and, over the years, reflected in countless conversations rooted in an ever-deepening culture of integrity, trust, communication, and the growth and development of their individual people. The inkjet division, led by General Manager Greg Merten, has left behind a legendary legacy for HP.

PART II

Awakening Your Sacred Listening for Yourself

Our deepest fear is not that we are inadequate. Our deepest fear is that we are powerful beyond measure. It is our light, not our darkness, that most frightens us. We ask ourselves, 'Who am I to be brilliant, gorgeous, talented, fabulous?' Actually, who are you not to be? You are a child of God. Your playing small doesn't serve the world. There's nothing enlightened about shrinking so that other people won't feel insecure around you. We are all meant to shine, as children do. We were born to make manifest the glory of God that is within us. It is not just in some of us; it is in everyone, and as we let our own light shine, we unconsciously give others permission to do the same. As we are liberated from our own fear, our presence automatically liberates others.

Marianne Williamson,
A Return to Love

CHAPTER 14

Integrity

Creating Wholeness and Completion

As we saw in Chapter 13, by having the courage to speak and listen with courage and compassion, Dale stepped into his leadership and began forging and creating a space of completion that had not been there before. He created a safe space—a place in which each person was freed up to speak what was hard for each of them to say without fear of repercussions. Listening happened, sacred listening, listening from his heart to theirs.

Listening for completion, listening for wholeness.

I know that may sound weird. However, think about it: when something is complete, it is entire, it is harmonious, it is whole.

The condition and environment Dale created for his team allowed for a fresh start, a new beginning, and the forging of a future that would have been impossible to achieve if there had been no honest communication.

He could "hear" the absence of communication, and people on his team were suffering. When communication is not present, nothing works.

To listen with and for integrity is a very powerful level of listening, one that creates wholeness and completion.

What is integrity?

Integrity refers to the wholeness, soundness, or fulfillment of something. When something has integrity, it is complete and unbroken; life is satisfying.

I also hear the word "harmony" in this. Dale was committed to restoring harmony among the department's members. That harmony allowed for coordinated action within the department and even between department members and the external world.

Integrity serves as a foundation that allows life to work for us. And in the absence of integrity, people suffer.

Without integrity, things just plain don't work.

I once heard a story about integrity. Imagine this: you are at the front of a small boat with a team of rowers, calling the shots and keeping them all rowing together. Suddenly, water starts filling the boat. Clearly, you can't just keep rowing with water filling the boat. So, you quickly give everyone a pail to bail the water out. They bail, but the water keeps coming in. So, you shout: "Bail harder!"

Still, the water pours in. You yell once more, a bit louder, "Bail harder! Bail faster! Bail more!"

The water keeps coming into the boat. Everyone keeps bailing water frantically.

Finally, someone notices that there is a hole in the bottom of the boat. At full volume, he yells, "We have a hole! Let's stop bailing and plug the hole!"

Creating and restoring integrity is like that. There are holes at the bottom of our boats. And, even after we plug up the existing holes, life seems to serve us up with opportunities to create more holes.

Therefore, we must remain attuned to the presence of our integrity holes, or the areas where our integrity is lacking.

The good news is it's always possible to plug up the holes. It's possible to increase the degree of integrity in your life. When you do, you will experience greater ease, velocity, the possibility of building a new future, the potential for productivity that wasn't available to you before, and the possibility of a newfound sense of peace.

But first, you must identify the holes.

For example, where your values and your actions are inconsistent, there is a cost to your integrity.

Where word and deed (what you promise and how you act) don't match up, there is a cost to your integrity.

When someone breaks their word and does not acknowledge it, trust in the relationship breaks down.

Restoring integrity becomes critical. I call that "cleaning up after a breach."

I offer this not as a morality conversation but more as a "way life works" conversation.

I would go so far as to say that when you are a leader with integrity, when your orientation in life focuses on workability and empowerment, and when you are committed to making life work for everyone, a condition of integrity is necessary for producing results. It serves as a foundation.

Integrity comprises the building blocks of that foundation.

One little item, one that goes unseen and therefore not caught, makes it very difficult to clean up a condition of low integrity: instead of acknowledging that we have not kept our word, we give our reasons or justifications instead. We blame something outside of our control.

I have found that you and I *either* follow through, keeping our word, *or* we have reasons, justifications, explanations, and stories for *why* we did not keep our word.

Instead of taking responsibility, we live in our story; we live in our reasons. That's like shoving everything under a carpet so we don't have to see it. Very soon, it leaves us standing, or, rather, wobbling, on top of an unstable mound instead of a strong foundation of completion, firmness, stability, and grounding.

Creating this strong foundation often requires completing something from our past so our present and future can be free and not colored by the past. Usually, a revisitation of the past is called for.

Here's an example: Sometime during the mid-1980s, I led a course for dentists only, put together by a dentist friend of mine who practiced in

New Orleans. He knew many dental practitioners and wanted to share this powerful work with his friends. The course was held in Slidell, Louisiana.

Near the beginning of the program, I asked participants to share what they intend to gain from it. Tom was the first to speak. He had brown hair with a touch of gray at the edges. With sadness in his voice and a frown on his face, he revealed that he was in a conundrum; he was taking the course to decide whether or not to quit his practice after twenty years in business. I asked him to provide us with a bit more information, and he said his practice wasn't satisfying and that he didn't have many patients. I inquired how long this had been the case. He replied that it had been about fifteen years. Later in the course, I asked him what had happened fifteen years ago. He said, "Nothing."

I let it rest, knowing the truth would reveal itself to him at some point later.

It did. The next day, while we were exploring the depths of integrity to clear out the mud, he raised his hand high into the air, saying, "I remember now what happened fifteen years ago!"

Everyone sat up in their seats to listen. What had occurred? He had let himself become distracted during a root canal procedure and had given his patient a poor root canal. He knew it, yet he said nothing to her, allowing her to leave the office.

He felt terrible. Once she left, Tom's inner judge spoke up, pounded the inner gavel loudly three times, and said to him, "Shame on you! You can't count on yourself to take care of your own patients. You'd better not *ever let* your practice grow."

So be it!

Verdict? Guilty! Punishment: a small, unsatisfying practice.

I asked Tom if he would be willing to forgive himself. He said, "Absolutely not."

We talked for a long time, and I drew many distinctions around forgiveness, which freed him up to grant himself that gift and, ultimately, let go of the blame, shame, and guilt he had been holding against himself for years like a cudgel. We will be talking more about forgiveness in Chapter 16.

After three sequential days of the course, everyone returned home to live their lives out of their newly created stands for a new future, with new goals and projects.

Three weeks later, participants returned for days four and five of the course, having "been in life" for a while.

Tom had acquired six new patients during the three-week period.

Everyone wanted to know where he had advertised. He hadn't.

He had done some research and found the phone number of the previously mentioned root canal patient. That had been his project. He called her.

After a few rings, he heard a voice: "Hello?"

There she was! He said, "Hello, Mrs. so and so. I don't know if you remember me. I'm your former dentist."

"Oh, yes," she said, rather coldly. "I remember you quite well."

Tom shared with us that he said something like, "Well, I know this is really late for me to be making this call to you, but I wanted to call you to say I am so sorry for that day, many years ago, in my office, when I gave you a bad root canal and didn't let you know. I am so sorry, both for having done that and for not telling you. I want to apologize to you now, even though it's years later."

Pause.

She said, "I knew right away. That's why you never saw me again."

He repeated how sorry he was.

And then, again, a long pause.

"I must say, your calling me is quite a surprise," she said.

Another pause, as she thought about it more.

"That's quite a thing for you to do. In a way, it restores my trust in the whole dental profession, which I had lost. Thank you very much for calling me."

And they got off the phone.

Tom said he felt relieved and lightened up as if a heavy load had lifted from his mind and his life.

He also shared with us that many of the patients he saw in that three-week period commented on how happy he seemed, some even asking if something had happened to lift his spirits.

Within a week of his "root canal" call, new patients had begun making appointments. He had no idea if this ex-patient had anything to do with it, but he did know that somehow, he had plugged a hole.

CHAPTER 15

Deepening Integrity in Your Life

Having Integrity Be Your Foundation

Now is *your* chance to strengthen the integrity of your life and your relationships with yourself and others.

I invite you to participate in an exercise designed to support you in rebuilding your foundation of integrity.

We will list all the conceivable places in your life where integrity could be missing. To complete this exercise, spend time with each question and write down what you see without censoring or monitoring yourself. Ask yourself the question or read the listing two or three times. If nothing comes up after you read an item on the list, that's fine; don't worry about it. When something does show up for you, just write down what comes to you and then ask again.

Spend thirty seconds to three minutes on each item.

Don't let your mind get in the way or overthink it, and don't tell yourself you don't really need to write it down. Just write it down! And, of course, you don't have to show or share this list with anyone unless you want to.

And don't worry about what we're going to do with the list. We'll work with your list afterward, on your behalf, creating a new condition of completion in your life. These incompletions will open a new universe of possibilities where you can grant yourself some new endings. From that place, you can create a new beginning—a much more fulfilling and meaningful future.

You could consider this exercise as the start of reconnecting with your own sacred listening for your Self, your integrity and alignment, and reawakening to your sacred nature.

"For only with completion can a new beginning start," as I said in a poem called "For Giving Endings," in my previous book, *Crossing Thresholds, Island Reflections.*

Okay. Are you ready? Grab yourself a pen and a piece of paper, and let's begin.

Let's call this list: "Areas in My Life in Which Integrity Can Be Increased."

Areas in My Life in Which Integrity Can Be Increased

- Places and ways I am not or have not been living or acting in accordance with my own values and principles
- Gossip: (Think! What have I said about someone that I would not say to them—that's gossip!)

    - People I have gossiped about

    - People I have gossiped with

    - Gossip I have witnessed

- Broken agreements, promises not kept that I have not communicated about (to myself, to others, others to me)
- Unexpressed or avoided communications
- Any associate, family member, friend, relative, customer, boss, former boss, colleague, employee, or company that I have a file on that I have been massaging

- Unacknowledged accomplishments (from others to you, from you to others, from you to yourself)
- Things I have wanted to be, do, or have related to work that have not come about (failed intentions, outcomes, purposes, unrealized visions)
- Resentments and regrets, what I feel guilty about, what I am ashamed of
- Any area of my life where I have not acted on what matters
- Anything Life is calling for me to be doing that I am not doing in the arenas of:

    - My health and well-being

    - Community

    - Family

    - Development/spirituality

    - Self-expression

    - Myself

    - My happiness

    - My freedom

To do this thoughtfully may take a while. It will be time well spent. When you are complete with your list, stop. Acknowledge and congratulate yourself, taking a deep breath.

Be with yourself and those items in a space of compassion and acceptance. Remember, you, too, are human! Notice if you feel stuck anywhere or if you're resisting being with any of the items or an experience that has come up, and just allow yourself to be with it for a minute or so. This isn't about guilt-tripping yourself; it's about completing those items and achieving an inner sense of freedom and peace in your life.

In the next chapter, we will access the key to allowing the past to remain in the past, not in the present or the future. We will gift ourselves with establishing a foundation of completion and integrity upon which we can build a heartful life—a life filled with meaning, passion, joy, commitment, and relationships that work (including the one with yourself!), and live a life that truly matters.

That key is forgiveness. Many of us have misunderstandings about what forgiveness truly means, which keep us from easily accessing it. Forgiveness becomes available once you free yourself from those misconceptions. And since "forgiveness is the key to happiness," a common saying, it's worthwhile taking a deep swim in those clear, cleansing, and purifying waters.

The Power of Forgiveness

From Suffering to Peace

In the space of forgiveness, peace begins.
In the space of forgiveness, happiness begins.
In the space of forgiveness, love begins.

A closed heart can become brittle, and brittle things break easily. An open heart is a beautiful, expansive bowl large enough to hold both joy and sorrow in equal measure. Sometimes, it can feel like a long journey from a closed heart to an open one.

If you've completed the work in the last chapter, you may now find yourself facing your incompletions, regrets, resentments, sadness, possible grief, and disappointment. The reawakening of unexpressed pain often arises with the journey of going deep.

In the presence of forgiveness, completion begins. Completion carves a path for new beginnings. It is a pathway for us to presence, to freeing ourselves from the past.

So, let us now dive deep into the lake of forgiveness, where its pure waters can cleanse our souls and act as a healing balm to our closed hearts, opening them.

My intention in these two chapters is twofold. One intention is to create space for you to give yourself the gift of forgiveness in the present and to heal what is currently incomplete in your life. My second intention is to provide you with deep and lasting access to forgiveness for the rest of your life, like an "arrow in your quiver" to use when you need it.

Forgiveness sets you free. It gives you the power to free yourself and others from the past and experience Peace.

Forgiveness is a source of power; a pathway for leading a freed-up life. It gives you the power to free yourself and others from the past and experience a sense of wholeness in the present.

We all have a longing for restoration, renewal, recovery, and providing ourselves with our own sacred listening. Even when we're off, even when we've made mistakes, we can give ourselves this precious gift.

You and others around you will make mistakes. We all need access to a restorative conversation to grant amnesty for our mistakes and failures; that amnesty opens the doors to compassion.

A young man in one of my courses, a man named Donnie, granted himself a deep level of amnesty and freed his life.

Donnie was in his late twenties, with dark hair and a slender frame. He never smiled, and he was known for that. Nobody had ever seen him smile—not since he had returned home from Iraq.

Donnie did the work on forgiveness in the course in a deeply meaningful way.

Afterward, he raised his hand, walked to the front of the room, and turned around to face the participants. He stood tall and shared:

"I signed up for the Army with my best friend. We were both sent to Iraq. We were happy about that. I was the platoon leader, and I was in the first tank.

"That day on patrol, my best friend said to me, 'I want to be in the first tank.'

"I said, 'No, no way!'

"My friend begged me. I kept saying 'no.'

"Finally, my friend said, 'Please, let's just flip a coin.'

"I relented. 'Okay,' I said. The quarter landed in the dirt. My friend won. He was in the lead tank, and I was in the second tank."

Choked up, and starting to get teary, with a haunted expression, Donnie haltingly said, "I watched the lead tank blow up as it hit an explosive device."

With great difficulty, he continued, "I jumped out and held him, cradling him, as he died in my arms."

All of us in the room were there with him on that field. We could feel what he felt and see what he was seeing.

The room was midnight quiet. Several people had tears in their eyes. One silently wept.

Donnie haltingly shared that he had kept the quarter in his pocket since then.

He wore his friend's dog tags.

He would not forgive himself. He had refused all those years.

He never smiled because he never let himself be happy.

He thought it would dishonor his friend if he were happy.

Then Donnie looked up towards his right as if he could sense his friend's presence. He said to his friend, with great love, in a quivering voice, "I forgive you for dying."

We could almost see his friend, invisible as he was.

As he stood there, tears streaming down his cheeks, he took a deep breath and said, in a strong, powerful voice, "Donnie, I forgive you for letting your friend get into that tank."

Then he wept for several moments right in front of the class. What a privilege it was to share those sacred moments.

Donnie speaking those words freed him.

I found out later that Donnie had been diagnosed with PTSD and had been through countless hours of therapy.

For years, no one knew how to cure it.

Three weeks later, at the next session of the course, Donnie shared with all of us that he had been smiling the whole time between days three and four. Other participants in the class, people who were co-workers with him, also spoke about that.

At the lunch break, he asked me if he could talk with me privately. Donnie reached into his pocket, offering me the quarter in that special moment, saying, "I don't need this anymore. I want you to have it."

I keep that quarter in a special heart-shaped box to remind myself of the power of forgiveness to set me free. It also reminds me of Donnie and the extraordinary gift he gave the planet—his freedom, love, and happiness—when he found the courage to forgive.

While this is Donnie's story, this is each of our stories as well. Forgiveness sets us free.

You can think of forgiveness visually as opening the palms of our hands from a clenched fist. When we are clenched, we hold on to our resentments, grievances, and grudges toward ourselves and others. Forgiveness is the act of opening that fist, letting go, and giving freely.

Or, you could think of it as an exchange: an exchange of resentment for freedom from a long-held breath, for being able to breathe freely again.

Sometimes, it's hard to open that clenched fist. It doesn't want to open. We think that if we continue to guard the wounds, they will heal . . . but they don't. Or we believe that if we hold on to our grudge, we are somehow "getting back at them." But we aren't.

And we stay stuck.

So, in a way, it's a giving up of a claim: the claim to punish, take revenge, or maintain your position of "I am right."

However, who suffers most in this scenario? We do. And we keep hurting ourselves.

The Buddha compared the lack of forgiveness to holding a hot coal in your palms, wanting to throw it at someone else, but it won't leave your hand. It clings to you, and in the end, you are the one who gets burned.

Here are three common misconceptions about forgiveness. Once you know them, you have easier access to its power.

1. People think forgiveness is a "copping out." That is a myth. Forgiveness is not copping out.

2. Forgiveness has nothing, absolutely nothing, to do with what someone does or does not "deserve." "They don't deserve it" is frequently the position people stay stuck in forever, keeping themselves chained to their blame, resentments, and grudges their whole lives.

Please let that sink in—consider the possibility of that. We think we'd be "copping out" if we forgave them "because they don't deserve it."

3. Last, to forgive does not mean to *condone*.

There are no behavioral strings attached. You can forgive someone without condoning what they did or didn't do, and you can call the police. You can forgive someone and choose not to stay married to them (as I did with my first husband).

You can forgive someone and choose not to work with them any longer, as I did with a previous business partner. You can forgive someone and choose not to see them anymore. You can forgive someone and let them go, or fire them. However, the conversation regarding the firing, for example, will contain honor, with intention and no attachment, ensuring that neither of you remains stuck with that final conversation, which, without forgiveness, could become an incident that haunts both of you in the future.

It is even possible to forgive your "enemies."

I read a life-altering story in Lynne Twist's extraordinary book, *Leading a Committed Life*. In it, she shares that she had the privilege of being present at Nelson Mandela's inaugural address, which was incredibly inspiring for everyone there.

While sitting between two members of royalty at the banquet after the address, Mandela asked them to move their chairs and invited the two men who had been his jailers during seventeen of the twenty-seven years he was imprisoned to take their seats next to him.

In the seventeenth year, he said, he realized that such hatred was unhealthy for him and was killing him, and he would not be able to free his people if he did not also free his oppressors. During that year of his imprisonment, he found a place in his heart for them. He learned about their families and their lives. He said that year, he started running the Movement for Freedom from prison.

Once his jailers were sitting at his table, he introduced them to everyone present. Then, he turned around, faced them, and said, "Please forgive me for my years of hatred for you."

With tears streaming down their faces, they asked him to forgive them for everything they had done to him.

You might want to pause here and think about that.

Here is another story, my own, with another great Being on the planet.

In 1994, my husband and I attended a five-day retreat with 1,500 participants, led by the Dalai Lama at a hotel conference center in Arizona. The theme of the retreat was "Patience." We had the privilege of being in the presence of the Dalai Lama, who radiated joy and warmth, for six hours each day through meditation, readings, teachings, and question-and-answer sessions. Each night, after dinner, we watched videos showing the Chinese causing havoc and violence in Tibet.

On the third day of that session, during a Q&A session, a young man asked the Dalai Lama a question that had also come to my mind.

"Your Holiness," he said. "Each day, you lecture us about patience. Each night, we watch these videos of what the Chinese are doing to your country, raping your country. What are we to do with this? How can you exercise patience against your enemies?"

The Dalai Lama's face contorted. He appeared puzzled and confused. He remained that way for about two minutes.

Finally, his face brightened into a broad smile. With wide, sparkling eyes and that face-crinkling grin, he said, at last, "My enemies? Oh! You must mean *my teachers!*"

Silence. Silence in the hall while we all took that in.

That was astounding. That put a different framework around everything, casting a different light on everything and opening each of us to a new possibility. I asked myself:

Who could I now regard as a teacher who "feels like" an enemy?

What am I being taught?

Perhaps the most challenging circumstances and complex emotions that are triggered by our "enemies" become nutrient-rich soil that transforms our lives and allows us to find richness and spiritual growth.

How do I access forgiveness?

When you truly let go of anger and resentment, releasing it entirely, forgiveness appears. Although the clouds sometimes hide the sun's brightness and warmth, the sun is always present. So is forgiveness. You've just blown the clouds away.

Grace appears when you let go of your blame and resentment.

I also invite you to consider this: there is a benefit in *not* forgiving.

Holding on to the blame and the resentment lets you "off the hook." Like you have nothing to do with it.

Holding on to blame and righteousness also costs you.

It costs you your happiness.

A well-known phrase is "Forgiveness is the key to happiness." When I first heard that, I thought, *Yes, but people are more interested in playing the victim and being right than in being happy.* The evidence is that people are very reluctant to give up suffering. After all, we get a lot of satisfaction from feeling sorry for ourselves. We don't have to take responsibility!

Many people's gravestones could read, "I died, but I was right!"

Look for yourself: what is the cost? You will see it costs you your voice, power, freedom, peace, relationships, and, ultimately, the opportunity to be the creator and author of your own life.

When the past keeps repeating in different forms, as it does without forgiveness, the cost is your ability to author a new future, a new life for yourself, a life of your own choosing.

We are willing to sing the song "They Done Me Wrong" our whole lives.

One of my previous teachers, a man named Brian Regnier, brilliantly introduced this simple question to me many years ago: "How long are you willing to suffer?"

He also asked the question, "How good are you willing to have it be?"

I pondered those questions for a long time and still do, regularly. They make my heart glad; they allow me to leap into my own soaring spirit.

These questions I invite you to ask yourself now.

I have introduced many important distinctions about forgiveness in this chapter. To repeat a few key points:

- Forgiveness is unconditional and has nothing to do with deserving or condoning. The one who gets freed up around forgiveness is you.
- Forgiveness sets you free to invent a new conversation that makes a difference.
- Forgiveness is an intentional letting go.
- There are huge "payoffs" to not forgiving, but they come at even huger costs.

What are the payoffs?

You get to be "off the hook," and, of course, you get to be right, which is intrinsic, like an addiction, to the human mind. The mind or the ego just *loves* to be right. We'd rather be right than anything!

What are the costs?

Your relationship, your power, your freedom, your health, your well-being, your productivity, your peace, and building a culture of trust around you.

If you look carefully, you will see that the cost of withholding your forgiveness outweighs the payoff in each case.

Try this on, personally. Do the work.

Joan Borysenko, Ph. D., a cancer cell biologist and licensed psychologist, frequently shares how resentment poisons our minds and occupies our thoughts. She says:

> *It is a powerful adversary that keeps us from being fully present in the moment. As long as we are shackled by hatred or judgment, we cannot claim the true power of our mind to heal. We are prisoners of the past.*

I was in a workshop where Joan told us a story about a moment in which her relationship with her mother had been transformed. It was shortly before her mother died. She started the story by saying, "The holiest ground is where an ancient hatred becomes a present love."

Joan shared with us that she had a complicated relationship with her mother throughout her life.

When it was time for her mother to pass on, she was in the hospital with her family gathered around her. It was clearly time for her to die. The technicians took her out of her room and wheeled her in a gurney to the bowels of the hospital. She was gone for a long time, and the family sent Joan down to find her. Joan located her in the basement of the hospital. She started to wheel her back up to the room, but a medical technician stopped her and said they had to wait for the diagnosis.

Her mother said, "I'm dying, you idiot! How's that for a diagnosis?"

Joan halted in the midst of her story. Once the audience's laughter subsided, she said dryly, "That'll give you some idea of her general personality," and resumed her narrative.

A few minutes later, Joan and her mom found themselves in the elevator together. About that moment, Joan says, "We accomplished the work of a lifetime when she looked up at me with her clear, blue eyes and said, 'I've made a lot of mistakes. Would you forgive me?'"

Then, Joan expressed it like this: "The difficulties of a lifetime vanished in the magic of that moment . . . Sometimes, the most problematic relationships are, unbeknownst to us then, holy ground being tilled."

I express it like this: after a lifetime of struggle with her mother, a sacred listening was born.

For truly, what good does holding on to resentment do? We often mistake righteous anger for power when, in reality, holding onto that anger prevents us from opening our hearts to others. When we are in an open-hearted state of compassion, we are happy. We are free. And we naturally transmit this energetic state to others.

"*Tsewa*," it's called in the Tibetan language; a heart full of tenderness. And, in that tenderness, we, and our relationships, are healed.

Creating Space
for the Rest of Your Life

Forgiveness is the Key

Forgiveness is not an occasional act;
it is a permanent attitude.
Martin Luther King, Jr.

Diane Merten knew this. She not only "knew this," but lived this.

Diane was married to my client, Greg Merten, the general manager of the inkjet business at Hewlett-Packard, when I worked with them.

Because the HR manager of the business also served as the chair of the school board, we once hosted a course for the school district's parents and leaders. Corvallis was a small town where everyone knew each other. The Mertens were well respected in their community for their dedication to a life of service and caring.

Diane was the epitome of heart-in-action and profoundly generous: generous of heart, generous of mind, generous of body, and generous of spirit—a deeply good person.

Diane and Greg's third son, Scott, was killed in an automobile accident in 1990 at only sixteen years old.

Scott's friend Jason was driving the car and came through the accident unscathed.

Diane learned about Scott's death through a visit from a highway patrolman, who came to her door after midnight. Diane was alone in her house. Her husband was on a business trip in Singapore.

What she said was, her whole body shaking, "At first, after the shock, I found myself so angry at the driver of the car, I was in a rage. I couldn't even access my grief. I knew I had to go to work within myself to get through the anger, to be able to start to process the grief.

"I was up all night, working with myself and my anger. I never slept at all.

"I was able to go deep and do the work that allowed me to access my grief. And, I was finally able to begin grieving deeply.

"The next afternoon, around 3:30 p.m., there was a knock at my door. Greg was not yet home. I opened the door.

"There stood a young man, another friend of Scott's. His whole body was shaking. He asked to come in. Of course, I said, 'Yes,' and opened the door wide.

"He was tense and fearful. Trembling, his eyes wide and pleading simultaneously, he said to me, almost crying, 'All day at school, we've been dividing into camps. There's been the Scott camp and the Jason camp. The other kids asked me to come to see you. We want to know what you are going to do about Jason.'

"And because of the work I had done on myself, I was able to put my arms around this young boy's shoulders, hold him tight, and say into his ear, 'I am not going to do anything about your friend but love him.'

"This boy's body crumbled to the floor, weeping. When he could stand again, he said the deepest thank you and, referring to the camps, said that there could now be healing."

When Diane shared the story in the room, which was filled with the parents in that community, almost everyone was crying and dabbing their eyes. One person raised her hand, stood, and said, "We were doing the same thing. You healed the whole community."

Perhaps take a pause, for a moment, just thinking about that.

There's one more part to this story. Thirty years later, a friend visited Diane. They were in the kitchen, where a moldy pie —the "evidence"—sat on the counter. She was complaining about a moldy pie someone had left out. Diane heard the doorbell ring. She excused herself and went to the door. Standing there was Jason, trembling. He said, "I just want to see someone I know who loves me."

They hugged tightly. Diane said, "I am so glad you know I love you." Jason smiled and left.

When she returned to the kitchen, her friend was crying. "Here I am, grousing about a moldy pie, and you can hug the boy that was responsible for your son's death."

I was profoundly moved when I heard that first story in that room, and I returned to my own list of incompletions. While I am committed to not processing personally when I am leading, I couldn't help myself. I quickly assessed my own incompletions (resentments and regrets) at the time and, like Diane's friend, saw how petty they were.

That course and Diane's courage, open-heartedness, and grace became a clarion call for me and for all of the participants to enter a new level of my journey of living from forgiveness.

I invite you to do this work, now, for and with yourself.

Go back over your list of incompletions, one at a time, and allow whatever emotions are associated with each incompletion to come up. Just notice them and let them be. Then see if you would be willing to forgive yourself or someone else.

If you are willing, place a check mark in the margin. If not, feel free to skip it. This will indicate what to focus on next as you make this your own.

Give yourself whatever time you need to complete this work. Once you've completed it, we'll proceed to the next step.

Making This Your Own

You can do this exercise in three ways, and you can go back and forth between the ways.

This is a traditional methodology called Gestalt, designed by Fritz Perls, that I have used.

It may sound a bit strange to you, but it works if you allow yourself to get into it.

If you remember the story about Donnie and his best friend going to Iraq with him, this was the exercise that made such a difference in Donnie's life.

You can do this with your eyes open or closed.

Way #1

Imagine the person you want to forgive sitting across from you. You are both there, and fully present, intending to be in communication.

Having let go of your resentment, say to this person, with your heart open, and meaning it:

"(Name): I forgive you for . . . ."(and say what you forgive them for).

Let yourself get into it. If you have not fully let go of your anger, do so as if you are speaking with the person. Open your heart.

Then, let them say back to you, "Thank you," having accepted your words. If there is anything else they would like to say to you in their forgiveness, please accept what they have to say with an open heart.

If you have a friend who is also reading this book, you could do the exercise in person with each other, choosing an A and a B, with A speaking first, and B being the person being spoken to.

Way #2

You could also say to this person

"(Name), please forgive me for . . . ."

And let them say back to you, "I forgive you."

And then go on to the next person on your list.

Way # 3

Also (*and this is important*), imagine yourself, at least once, as the person sitting across from you. Forgive yourself, (calling yourself by your name) either: "(Your name), I forgive you for . . . ."

Or "(Your Name,) please forgive me for . . . . . ."

You could do the entire exercise just that third way, forgiving yourself.

Take as much time as you need.

When you have completed this exercise, reflect on the following questions. You might also want to journal.

Address: What has just opened for me? Look at, see, and then write what has opened up.

And address the question, "What is present in the presence of forgiveness?"

Write down what you have just said to yourself.

Take a deep breath.

Please know that you do not need to communicate anything to anyone; this work was for you with you. At the same time, you may want to open up a conversation with someone else. That is wholly up to you.

You will find that if you have authentically forgiven yourself and/or another, you are standing in front of nothing. Literally nothing.

You have given yourself the freedom and opportunity to create a (new) future worth living for.

The opportunity to create, like for an artist, requires standing before a blank canvas, not a full one. It is not a reworking of the past; it lives in nothingness, zero.

And from nothing, you can invent. If you are an author, it's like a pen poised over an empty page.

"What," you may ask, "is the secret to inventing, creating, and authoring your life?"

That is a big question, for there is a key and one that you will discover, distinguish, and apply to your own life in the next chapter.

CHAPTER 18

The Secret Key to Inventing Your Future

Taking a Stand

Now that you have entered the healing world of forgiveness, you most likely find yourself at a new beginning. You stand in front of a life where you can live free from the grip of the past while still honoring it. Forgiveness has set you free, and now what was incomplete in the past is no longer incomplete and does not need to extend into the future. You are whole, and the future is a spacious new opening.

As I said in the last chapter, it is as though you are an artist standing in front of a blank canvas or an author looking at a blank white page of a book she or he is writing. You can hear new and larger horizons beckoning you if you listen deeply enough. You can ask for inner wisdom to light your way.

What is the new horizon in me that wants to be seen?

You can hear, create, and live the future that is now calling to you.

These next two cuts offer further and deeper insights into integrity as a key principle in leading your life from sacred listening, from being at one with yourself, with others, with Life itself, and with Source, or the Great Mystery, or the Creative Energy of the Universe—whatever you want to call that Spark of Aliveness, that place where you are Whole.

Parker Palmer says in his essay, "The Heart of a Teacher," "Integrity requires that I discern what is integral to myself selfhood, what fits and what does not—and then I choose life-giving ways of relating to the forces that converge within me: do I welcome them or fear them embrace them or reject them move with them or against them? By choosing integrity, I become more whole, but wholeness does not mean perfection. It means becoming more real by acknowledging the whole of who I am."

So that leads us to the question, "Who am I?"

This was the question, if you recall, with which I began my own life's journey of growth and development.

Now, we address that question through two paths, both of which will allow you to create a future worth living—one that grants you aliveness and is entirely your own.

One question is, *Who am I as a unique contribution on the planet?*

The second question is, *What do I stand for?*

PART I: WHO AM I AS A UNIQUE CONTRIBUTION?

Let us begin with a dive into your unique contribution. This work is an opportunity to deepen your relatedness and your sacred listening for yourself.

To drop your files on yourself.

To embody that you are deeply worthy and also deeply loved.

To own your own wisdom, beauty, and magnificence, along with your place in the universe.

You can ask yourself, *Who am I as a unique contribution?*

So often, we spend our hours and our days trying to be someone else or wishing to have the life circumstances of someone else—someone who may not even be alive, or someone who is famous. I know, for a while, I did: *If only I could write as well as . . .* or *if only I could contribute to as many people as . . .*

I started to get suspicious of the "if only" conversation. I saw that so many of us live in this conversation. *If only I had that job, or that amount of money, or that partner, then I'd be happy.*

Buying into that conversation as though it were real left me feeling discounted, disconnected, and disenfranchised.

And so, we change jobs, we change circumstances, and we change partners while still carrying the "if only" conversation inside ourselves, thinking something else or someone else outside of us will make us happy, will fill that spiritual void.

And, when we do make a change, nothing *really* changes, for the real conversation is the internal one.

That spiritual void can be filled by awakening your awareness, realizing that while you *have* reactions, you are *not* your reactions, and the "I'm not worthy" song inside your head is not worthy of being sung.

That spiritual void can be filled through stand-taking, through listening for your own "enoughness," listening for the realization that you are not only worthy but also already loved. It is a profound listening for yourself: *I am enough. I am whole.*

As Marianne Williamson asks in *A Return to Love, Reflections on the Principles of a Course in Miracles,* "Actually, who are you not to be? You are a child of God. Your playing small does not serve the world . . . As we're liberated from our own fear, our presence automatically liberates others."

When I finally became content with myself and allowed myself to experience that I am loved, just as I am, with all my quirks, failures, and imperfections, as well as my talents and gifts, I found that I belonged and that even my flaws contributed in some way. After all, all of us are human. We are all part of the same journey, the journey of coming into our own authenticity. Once I gave up trying to be someone else, someone I was not, and owned that I was fine just the way I was and was not, Peace entered my heart.

Here is how one of my dear friends, James Bailey, and someone who has worked with me for thirty years, speaks of this same realization in his own life:

I used to think my life was my life circumstance.

I was a pudgy, acne-prone middle child who lived in the shadow of my older brother, who was most things I wanted to be: taller, smarter, popular, and athletic. I spent my childhood and early adult years trying to earn the respect of others through my "doings." By working hard, accomplishing business goals, and striving to win golf tournaments, my identity was sourced from my accomplishments (my doings), and my worth was sourced from how my accomplishments stacked up against others. The first time I truly looked inward and considered who I was in the matter of my life was in my first Heart of Leadership course in 1997. I confronted the questions: "What do I stand for?" and "What is my unique contribution to the world?"

These two essential questions have nothing to do with my doings, my older brother, my family of origin, or, quite frankly, my life circumstances. They have everything to do with me. Simply, me. These questions sparked an awakening and have been the source of an internal journey over the twenty-five years since The Heart of Leadership course.

And then he said, "One of my stands back in 1997 was 'I touch the lives of others.'"

"I touch the lives of others." What a powerful stand! This was a declaration, a stand, that emanated from James, realizing that *was* his unique contribution.

Before we turn it over for you to engage with this question through your own work, I want to conclude with two beautiful quotes. The first is from Dawna Markova in her book, *Wide Open: On Living with Passion and Purpose.* In it, she says:

Another thing I know is that we all need inspiration now. In times of great change, people reach for meaning because meaning brings strength. When we don't have a sense of purpose, when we don't know what we love, what gifts we bring, and what we truly serve, we create lives and workplaces that are fundamentally meaningless and devoid of vitality. We stop listening to the deepest aspects of ourselves and each other. We stop learning how to fill ourselves from the ordinary events of our lives. We become solitary bystanders rather than full participants in life.

And here is Mark Nepo, on the same theme, from his *The Book of Awakening: Having the Life You Want by Being Present to the Life You Have:*

Part of the blessing and challenge of being human is that we must discover our own true God-given nature. This is not some noble, abstract quest, but an inner necessity. For only by living in our own element can we thrive without anxiety. And since human beings are the only life form that can drown and still go to work, the only species that can fall from the sky and still fold laundry, it is imperative that we find that vital element that brings us alive.

Making This Your Own

To begin to dive into your own unique contribution, I invite you to these questions:

- What is my unique contribution?
- What am I reliable for contributing?
- What is the "vital element" that brings me alive?
- What lives at the core of my heart's desire?
- What gives me meaning?
- What gives me a sense of purpose?
- What do I love?

These are big questions.

To inspire your thinking, I'd like to share two practices or exercises that you could "try on" to address these questions.

Practice #1

Close your eyes. As you reflect, meditate, and delve beneath the surface of things, hold two or three ways of participating in life that give you a sense of vitality.

Inhale deeply and exhale as you experience yourself participating in them. What feelings arise in your heart? Allow yourself to embrace that joy, that sense of aliveness. What uniquely brings joy to your spirit?

When you open your eyes, take a pen in hand and start writing without censoring anything. Just brainstorm. It can include the music you love that makes you feel alive, as well as the type of environment that inspires you. What transports you to awe and wonder? Is it being present with nature? Walking in the rainforest? Eating? Gardening? Listening to certain music? Playing a musical instrument? Singing? Writing? Cooking? Birdwatching? Reading? Poetry?

I invite you to take some time writing without censoring yourself. What lights up your life? You are casting a wide net.

Practice #2

What do your earliest memories reveal to you as clues around the purpose of your life—that singular thread that runs through your life that can act as a homing device for your spirit and your life?

If you go deep enough, this gives you clues.

As an example, one of my earliest memories, and I can still see it as vividly as a movie in vibrant color, was, in my imagination, reading to a group of children who were sitting in a semicircle, mouths agape, interested, fascinated, and unabashedly tuned in to what I was saying. I was contributing to their lives, to their learning.

That memory revealed to me the essence of my purpose. I have always known I wanted to be a teacher. My teaching has taken many forms, ranging from being a public high school English teacher, to collaborating with health professionals to expand their practices, to teaching meditation, to leading programs that create transformations in people's lives, to transforming the culture of organizations and the people within them. It has all been "teaching"—and what I consider my purpose on this planet: to awaken others to their own hearts, their own wisdom, their Awareness, that which gives a direct experience of the eternal and of belonging.

As Howard Thurman asks:

> *Don't ask what the world needs. Ask yourself what makes you come alive and then go do it. Because what the world needs is people who have come alive.*

PART II: WHAT DO I STAND FOR?

Now, allow the work you have just done to provide fodder for your next piece, addressing the age-old question, "Who am I?"

That question offers an opportunity to deepen your capacity to lead an authentic life while opening up the opportunity to create your future.

The question could be stated another way: What do I stand for?

In *The Empowered Manager*, Peter Block comments: "The most fundamental choice we make is to create a future of our own choosing. In some ways, the future is the cause of our current behavior."

What does Block mean by this?

And the response to that question leads us to explore, distinguish, and then design one of the greatest secrets for living a life worth living: stand-taking.

Viktor Frankl, a survivor of Auschwitz, wrote a book called *Man's Search for Meaning*. In it, he interviewed other survivors to see if they shared any common experiences. Interestingly, they did. Frankl noted that everyone who survived felt they had something significant to accomplish in the future.

Think about that for a moment.

My daughter asked me, when she was eight years old, ruminating about this, "I wonder what it would be like to live if you felt you had nothing to live for in the future. And then, what if we did have something to live for?"

The question, "What is the future you stand for?" is a big question, a worthwhile question, a question to address with great fervor, interest, and rigor, and with your heart, and your soul, and also, a question to ask over and over and over again as you move through life, and the challenges that all life brings.

What is a stand?

A stand is a declaration, a kind of speaking in which your word and your being are one. That's called Integrity. That's called authenticity. In fact, while we spoke of Integrity earlier, I would go so far as to say that stand-taking is the ultimate integrity: integrity at the level of Being.

"Give me a place to stand, and I will move the Earth," the mathematician Archimedes said more than 2,000 years ago.

In Lynne Twist's book, *The Soul of Money*, she says, so beautifully:

> *I like to say that when we take a stand, we can move the world—the world of ideas and people who act on them. Taking a stand is a way of living and being that draws on a place within yourself that is at the very heart of who you are. When you take a stand, it gives you authenticity, power, and clarity. You find your place in the universe, and you have the capacity to move the world.*

So, stand-taking, your next opportunity, is an opportunity for you to give yourself authenticity, power, and clarity—to embrace your own capacity to move the world.

It all starts with listening—listening to your heart, listening for what wants to happen, listening for what calls you, listening for what would make your life worth living. You could say you are listening for the future that is calling, a future that speaks to you, sings to you, a future that you would love to create.

If you think back to why you got this book or what you wrote down when I asked you what was at stake as you read it, you were essentially creating a new possibility for yourself in the future.

What you said there. That is one of the areas in which you can take a stand.

Perhaps when you wrote down that possibility, it was a wish, a want, or a hope. Stand-taking shifts all that, transforming it from fingers crossed to "This is already so." A stand is a declaration from the future. It takes the idea out of hope and into "This shall be." In fact, it already is!

Leaders create futures by taking stands. The stand is who they are. The future—clearly created and clearly envisioned—is already who they are.

This is what Gandhi, who stood for a "free India before my death," meant when he said, "If we could change ourselves, the tendencies in the world would also change. As a man changes his own nature, so does the attitude of the world change towards him."

When my husband and I journeyed to Gandhi's ashram in India, the guide reaffirmed that this stand was always at the center of his presence whenever anyone came to meet him.

Martin Luther King, Jr.'s "I Have a Dream" speech embodied the presence and energy of the fulfillment of justice and equality.

Here are two keys to freedom for you on behalf of your work:

1. Stands do not need evidence for their validity. So don't go looking for evidence.

2. You do not need to know how you are going to fulfill your stand when you take your stand.

I like to say that first you take the stand, and then you dive off the high board, trusting that on your way down you will invent the water—the structure for fulfilling your stand.

This is important for you, as you can bring something into being that has never existed before you took that stand.

You start by honoring your word as yourself. That is your fundamental stand: I honor my word as myself. In other words, "I am my word. My word (the declaration I make) is who I am."

Stands give you access to creating your being, to creating yourself as a clearing for certain possibilities for the future. What is a clearing? The space for the existence of what you are standing for. For example, air is not a clearing for the possibility of a pen's function; a blank piece of paper is.

This is a domain in which words create a world to live in.

This is very distinct from wishing, wanting, hoping, or believing.

When an authentic stand is taken, the language shifts from plan to declaration. It shifts from "I would like to" or "we ought to" to "I stand for" or "I am committed to." The language you create shifts what you are working on from being a good idea to being the commitment that you are or the commitment that you stand for.

The stand is an act of courage, a saying so. We are waiting for someone to tell us what to do with our lives or how to improve. What is missing is that we don't deeply listen for what wants to happen, who we are in our sacred hearts, and let life shape itself.

When you take a stand, you partner with the universe. You listen deeply and trust the unfolding of the universe in whatever form it takes, letting go of any resistance that arises along the way to what is happening. You embrace what *is*. You provide Sacred Listening for what the universe calls for and the ways it offers its *gifts* to you, rather than *doing things to you*.

Here are a number of examples:

Gary Egan, who was a general manager at Hewlett-Packard, was dissatisfied with all the complaints going on in his organization. I witnessed him taking this stand:

> *I am committed to the idea that whenever someone leaves a conversation with me, they leave that conversation with more possibility than they had coming into the conversation.*

That stand is very powerful.

When I first moved to Bainbridge Island, Washington, from the Bay Area, my dear friend Ruth, who already lived there, asked me, "Have you been to the spiritual center of Bainbridge Island yet?"

I figured she was talking about a church. She wasn't. She was talking about a grocery store, Town and Country Market, in the center of our main neighborhood on the island.

I hadn't been there.

Later, I found out why it, in fact, *is* "the spiritual center of the island." Don Nakata, the CEO and one of the Nakata family owners of this store, said to me when I first met him, sharing about his vision: "We don't just sell groceries. We create community."

Now that's a stand. That stand is resonant with their mission: "Nourishing the quality of life." Wouldn't you love to shop at a store whose intention was to nourish the quality of your life through the food you eat?

A few years later, I saw that when the Bainbridge Island citizens voted for "Best place to meet people," you know who won? Yep, Town and Country Market!

Sometimes you must stand for something for a long time, even beyond your lifetime, before that stand is fully realized. For example, I stand for "the transformation of human consciousness is the source of healing for the planet."

Will that be fulfilled in my lifetime? I don't know. Still, that doesn't stop me from taking that stand.

The signers of the Declaration of Independence were clearing the way for the conversation, "All men are created equal." And they included a stand for life, liberty, and the pursuit of happiness: the foundation of our country.

> *We hold these truths to be self-evident," they said, "that all men are created equal, that they are endowed by their Creator with certain unalienable Rights, that among these are Life, Liberty, and the pursuit of Happiness.*

And a new country was born through language.

The tour guide told us that as each man went to sign the Declaration of Independence, they thought they were going to the gallows in doing so.

You could say, "I lead a life of integrity, where inner and outer are one."

A stand allows us to create a new future.

Part III: IN PREPARATION FOR MAKING THIS YOUR OWN

Now, it's (almost) your turn. The opportunity is about to be in your proverbial lap. Let me reiterate a few things to prepare you for your work, and then leave your life in your hands!

You can take a stand in any arena. Your stands can be philosophical or spiritual, practical or personal. They may be in any area of your life. For instance, some areas could include your family, parenting, community, specific individuals in your life, your work, your relationships, your well-being, operational stands, or stands regarding your organization. They might be in any aspect where you have felt blocked, halted, or unable to see any possibility.

They just need to be your own and matter to you.

Here are some examples of what I stand for in my own life in various areas.

Parenting

I stand for listening appreciatively to my daughter, getting into her world without judgment, and doing so in a way that makes her feel loved and known.

I stand for my daughter living in an environment that nurtures her, and in which her talents, creativity, and passion meet the world.

I stand for creating a new level of shared, mutual, and expressed connection.

Work

My courses and retreats, both online and live, and my interactions with others are sources of joy and aliveness in my own life and in the aliveness of others.

My writing reaches the hearts, minds, and consciousness of many, makes a difference in their lives and relationships, and expands the wakefulness of consciousness on the planet as a whole.

My work with organizations creates environments and cultures that promote strong collaboration, deep trust, and a sense of passion and purpose as they move their organizations forward.

Family

We delight in each other's company, each of us experiencing being empowered, supported, and appreciated.

We create environments that call for play, fun, and the pleasure of being together.

We support each other's well-being.

Development

I stand for ever deepening my listening for the Wise Guidance within.

I stand for Being Present.

My life is given over to Wonder, to Gratefulness, and to Awe.

Being of Service (Enlivening the World)

I am a stand for Sacred Listening as the source for healing relationships and having relationships work through time.

Mistakes and breakdowns are opportunities for growth, evolution, development, and profound new understandings.

I stand for the awakening of human consciousness as the source of healing for the planet in a world that works for everyone.

Making This Your Own

Okay!

I invite you to bring forth the possibility of yourself and the future. This moment is now yours.

Speak your heart; speak who you are. Take your time. Powerful stands come from sacred listening, which integrates you, others, and life.

Be with yourself and let yourself suggest to you what stands to take.

Be with yourself and listen for the future that is calling you.

You might write down your stands first, being with yourself and your heart. When you are complete, perhaps you will speak them aloud to yourself. Or you might find someone who knows you well and can be a sacred listener to your speaking.

And have fun.

To support you, here are some questions that can spark ideas for your stands.

- What are the horizons within me wanting to be seen, calling to me?
- What makes me feel alive?
- What did I write down that I wanted to accomplish, to open

up for myself, through reading this book? What stand could I take that would open up possibilities for me in that area?

- Who do I stand for being? Who am I, as a unique contribution on the planet?
- What is my purpose on the planet?
- What does my deepest being desire?
- What is the future that is calling?
- What do I stand for?

PART III
Awakening Your Sacred Listening for the World

Life will give you whatever experience is most helpful
for the evolution of your consciousness.
How do you know this is the experience you need?
Because this is the experience you are having at this moment.
Eckhart Tolle
A New Earth: Awakening to Your Life's Purpose

Stand-Taking as You Move through Life

Creating a New Future

I took a stand once that saved my life.

I call it "My Great Medical Adventure."

The time was spring 2003. The place: Seattle. My husband and I were in a hospital consultation room.

"For sure, you'll be losing your taste and smell," the young brain surgeon matter-of-factly said to me.

My husband and I, along with this white-jacketed doctor in his late thirties, stood in front of an image on an MRI. We could see a large blob, which he called a tumor, on a brown and white shadowed picture of my brain, which he called "the frontal lobe." He called it a "meningioma," a word unknown to me at that time.

He also said, "This will not be a walk in the park."

He said that, like five times, during this consultation. Maybe seven.

Whatever the number of times, I got it.

It—this surgery—would not be a walk in the park for him.

When we left his office, I walked out in a great deal of fear. Inside my head a single question kept rising – *Why me? Why me?*

For about four months, I had been experiencing a singular experience. At first, it only happened occasionally, and then more and more frequently: I completely forgot what I had been saying.

Not just a word, but the context as well, *of what* I had been talking about. Gone. It was all gone.

And then, after about two minutes, though it felt like a lifetime, my memory and what I had been wanting to express returned.

I had been attributing this experience to "senioritis"—you know, I thought I was becoming more forgetful as I aged. *Also,* since my husband, Don, was in the sixth year of his cancer treatments, these moments of forgetfulness that occurred from time to time seemed small and almost irrelevant, given what he was going through. So I wrote it off.

But when it happened when I was in front of a room, leading a course, I was 1) embarrassed, 2) concerned, and 3) frightened.

As Don was present as the logistics supervisor throughout the course, he was aware that these incidents had been occurring in my life. He calmed the room by standing at the back and telling the participants that I would be returning soon and that they should not worry.

And I did. Return soon.

"Get her to a doctor!" my father instructed Don during a phone call about a week later, when the same incident occurred.

We went, and after an EKG and an MRI, I found myself listening and trying in vain to absorb that I'd be losing my taste and smell after waking up from an absolutely necessary brain surgery that was "not going to be a walk in the park."

Such is life. As we move through life, expecting things to go according to our plans, sometimes the Universe intervenes. Our plans get upended. Whatever we thought was the direction we would take is no longer the path we are on. It's like driving down the road of life at seventy miles an hour and getting a flat tire. And this happens over and over again. You could call those moments breakdowns.

"Man plans, God laughs" is a common saying.

As I moved through this breakdown, I took strong stands—stands that gave me new openings into extraordinary breakthroughs as I hooked into the vital currents of life.

That first week, after leaving the "not a walk in the park" brain surgeon, I interviewed three other surgeons, all with greater experience than the first one. Each was very busy, made no personal connection with me, and showed no compassion or caring. While they were more confident about the surgery, they all predicted that I would lose my sense of smell and taste.

All that week, sensations of fear coursed through my body. They consumed me like a hungry monster from the deep. How could I lead a life without taste or smell? I tried to meditate, to embrace my fear, but I failed.

On the last day of the week, I had an appointment with my acupuncturist, Lois. She was not only a great practitioner but also very wise. She listened deeply.

When she heard the story of my symptoms, my diagnosis, and my saga of our consultations with the four brain surgeons, including the "this will not be a walk in the park" surgeon, she stopped. She went silent for quite a while. When, finally, she spoke, she said, "You know? Bodies have an intuitive wisdom. For your journey right now, this must be exactly what you need."

I came to a complete stop. Her words rang in my heart.

I repeated to myself what Lois had said to me. "For my journey, this must be exactly what I need."

This opened me up to a whole new world. Yes! Of course! For *my* journey, this *must* be exactly what I need!

Many years ago, I took a stand that all experiences, circumstances, or events in my life contribute to my consciousness, awakening, evolution, and development. This includes obstacles that appear as stops in my journey.

As soon as I took that stand, that "for my journey, this is exactly what I need," the anxiety and fear and their associated body sensations exited my body.

Lois had given me a key, a perspective that unlocked the door to being at peace.

By committing to and perceiving the Universe, including this, in that way, I quickly shifted my perspective regarding this breakdown. I transitioned from uncertainty to certainty, from fear to love, and from disaster to opportunity.

And then, Lois said, "You'll find the right surgeon."

"Oh, yes," I remembered. "I am committed to finding the right surgeon." Stand number two. I didn't know how to do that, but I knew I would.

I left Lois that day, at peace, seeing my whole life in a different light. I started thinking of the up-and-coming opportunity as "My Great Medical Adventure." That, too, was a stand.

There is a principle here, in stand-taking, which is absolutely essential, and such good news for us, expressed so beautifully by WH Murray:

> *Until one is committed, there is hesitancy, the chance to draw back, always ineffectiveness. Concerning all acts of initiative (and creation), there is one elementary truth, the ignorance of which kills countless ideas and splendid plans: that the moment one definitely commits oneself, then Providence moves too. All sorts of things occur to help one that would never otherwise have occurred. A whole stream of events issues from the decision, raising in one's favor all manner of unforeseen incidents and meetings and material assistance, which no man could have dreamt would have come his way. I have learned a deep respect for one of Goethe's couplets: "Whatever you can do, or dream you can, begin it. Boldness has genius, power, and magic in it."*

I had taken a stand, and Providence moved.

I saw that I had been operating inside a limiting belief—that I *had to* have the surgery in Seattle, close to home. After all, I had a five-year-old daughter, and it didn't occur to me that I could go anywhere else. I was a fly, caught in the spider's net of a paradigm.

I realized I needed to find the best brain surgeon possible. It didn't matter where I went—I could go anywhere; I just needed to find the right person. After all, this was a complex surgery, and my life was at stake.

Within that week, a friend of mine with whom my husband and I felt very comfortable offered to take care of our daughter while I was away.

I began my search for the right surgeon. I reached out to my network, and the same name repeatedly surfaced from various sources: Dr. Keith Black. He practiced at Cedars-Sinai Medical Center in Los Angeles, where he founded the Maxine Dunitz Neurological Institute. He was featured on the front cover of *Time* magazine and is widely regarded as one of the world's top brain surgeons.

I scheduled two appointments: one with Dr. Black and another with someone else at an institute in San Francisco.

We saw Dr. Black first. He greeted us (my husband was with me) in green surgeon scrubs. He was a handsome Black man, about six feet tall, with a round face and gentle brown eyes. Soft-spoken, he was casual, personable, friendly, and truly made an effort to connect with me as a person, not just a patient.

He was drinking a cup of coffee.

From the *Time* article, I knew that he performed operations in Beverly Hills, sometimes on well-known celebrities. I had expected the same kind of rushing through the consultation that I had been through before. This was different. He had plenty of time for me; as much time as I needed.

After studying the MRI, he completely grasped the situation. With warm eyes and a kind heart, he compassionately explained that the crucial aspect of the surgery was ensuring the tumor did not grow back. In other words, the entire tumor had to be removed. He noted that it would be a complex surgery.

I asked him, "Dr. Black, if you were in my position, consulting surgeons, what would you look for?"

He replied, "I'd seek a surgeon who has performed numerous brain surgeries and is an expert in the field, as you never know what you might encounter once you get into the brain."

I asked him how many brain surgeries he had performed. I can't remember what he said, but it was a very large number. I started to feel confident about this path.

But he hadn't mentioned losing my sense of taste and smell! Why not?

I told him, "Every other surgeon I consulted said that I would definitely be losing my taste and smell."

"Really?!" he exclaimed quizzically. "Hey, let's go into the next room and look at the MRI again." And we did.

He said, "Oh, I see. Your tumor is attached to both olfactory nerves."

Then he peered at the MRI further before continuing. He said, "I can save one of them, for sure, and you only need one."

And then he said, looking at me pointedly, "After all, you wouldn't want to stop having fine dining experiences with your husband, would you?"

That "cinched the deal." I felt like he knew me from the inside out.

I canceled my other consultation, and we set a date for the surgery for October 3 of that year.

Once I found the right surgeon, I felt unafraid. From that moment on, up until I was lying on the operating table, about to receive anesthesia, I remained unafraid. I certainly expected to feel fear, but I did not. I was at peace.

I had done everything necessary, and now I could "leave the rest to God."

Once I made my stand to find the right surgeon, I found the right surgeon. Once I trusted the surgeon, I trusted the Universe. Once I trusted the Universe, I had faith. Once I had faith, I knew it would all work out perfectly, however it worked out. I had no attachment to the outcome of the operation. I knew it would be what it would be, and I was okay with it. I could surrender.

Surrender is a path to inner peace.

When I heard the IV beep and opened my eyes in the ICU after the operation, Dr. Black was standing before me, coffee once again in hand. He looked at me. His first four words were, "We got it all."

Then he said, "Shut your eyes."

I shut my eyes, and the rich aroma of coffee wafted up my nostrils.

I am profoundly indebted to Dr. Black and the realm of Being of Service and healing from which he comes. His care was tangible. He was not merely a curer or a fixer; he was a healer. That was what I had been seeking, and that is why, despite their skills, those other surgeons did not appeal to me for collaboration.

Later, I discovered a book Dr. Black had written called *Brain Surgeon*. I discovered in the book this sentence:

> *Beyond knowing textbook neuroanatomy, neurophysiology, and techniques of neurosurgery, there is an energy, a spiritual flow between doctor and patient that is essential in an outstanding neurosurgeon. Patients may not always be able to articulate it, but they generally can feel this spiritual connection when it exists. This ability to merge your skill and expertise with your empathy and compassion is the key to becoming a thoughtful warrior in the brain. And, I would submit, without the mindset of the thoughtful warrior, it is very difficult to become an expert thief in the night.*

A week later, after the staples were removed, we flew home. The operation was on October 3. We flew home on October 10. On October 31, I had recovered enough to walk a mile to celebrate Halloween by trick-or-treating with my daughter. That was a miracle.

The recovery period took six months. During that time of reading, meditating, writing, and reflecting, I realized that I had a breakthrough to make in my relationship with my own work. My work, that of transforming people's lives and the culture of their organization, had always been powerful. Even with that, there was something missing for me—creativity, a fire, or a missing link to the wholehearted passion that allowed me to light myself up and light up the lives of the people in front of me at an unpredictable level.

It had been missing because the work I was doing was so powerful. Simply saying the words, alone and without being truly 100 percent present, led to remarkable results in people's lives. That extra spark of creating it, of full, wholehearted presence, added the kind of fire needed to take it over the top. The added dimension of deep rest and new insights into distinctions I had not noticed before, during this enforced reflection time, was the breakthrough I needed to move from outstanding to extraordinary. And personally? The dimension of joy, aliveness, and the resources available to me to serve others have been unparalleled.

The six-month recovery process created a forced "stop" in my daily actions. That time led to an extraordinary breakthrough in who I could be for people in my core work.

When I began leading again, I was astounded by the depth and power of the participants' breakthroughs. They experienced radical new openings in areas of their lives that had previously been problematic. They reported shifts in their consciousness from being asleep to awake, releasing states of negativity and reactivation. Their spouses and children were amazed by their profound appreciation and ability to listen. They healed relationships that had been broken and considered forever lost. They reconnected with their passion and discovered they could integrate their work and home life, leading whole-hearted lives. They found themselves at a new level of mentoring others and making a meaningful difference in the lives of those around them.

On a personal level, my experience of leading was like nothing I had experienced before. The level of love, delight, laughter, creativity, and connection that I felt, the pleasure that I felt, the privilege and blessing to lead that I felt, and the joy that I felt came from another level of leading—another, higher consciousness.

I discovered that, for my body at this stage in my life, navigating this passage was *exactly* what I needed. I needed that "Great Medical Adventure."

It all began with three simple stands—stands which I took after my visit to Lois, stands that reframed an experience of threat and fear into a Life-Giving breakthrough:

"For my journey right now in life, this is exactly what I need."

"I am committed to finding the right surgeon."

"My Great Medical Adventure provides the fertile soil for giving birth to an astonishing, joyous, new level of Creativity, Originality, Presence, Power, and Wisdom in contributing to the awakened lives of human beings and the evolution and wakefulness of consciousness on the planet."

Sometimes the struggle is exactly what we need.

CHAPTER 20

Creating a Sacred Listening for Life

Transforming Your Relationship to Problems and Breakdowns

As you have seen in the previous chapter, the turning point, the transformational shift for me was shifting from living in fear to embracing life as an adventure, with courage, acceptance, and surrender guiding the way. Since that pivotal moment when Lois said, "You know? Bodies have intuitive wisdom. For your journey right now, this must be exactly what you need," my life has not been the same.

Up until then, I had been in a deep reactive mode, replaying the audio track in my head: "You have a brain tumor," "This will not be a walk in the park," and "You will be losing your taste and smell." The visuals of not being able to enjoy the food I would eat for the rest of my life were terrifying, echoing down the long and fright-filled corridors of my mind.

"Words create worlds," Rabbi Abraham Heschel said.

Lois's words propelled me into another world, a world where my significant challenge transformed into an immense opportunity. Instead of being a source of upset and disruption, the passage became an opening to a profound journey, an adventure that would allow me to transform both myself and my experience of life. It was an occasion for wholehearted work, serious reflection, and deep thinking that would ultimately contribute to the rest of my life.

So, let's dive into the inner work I had done before that moment when Lois spoke—work that enabled me to immediately accept what Lois was saying and provided access to a dramatic shift that you can now experience. This work will also offer you the same opportunity: the ability to move from fear to peace. It will empower you to transform breakdowns into learnings and provide the capacity to turn breakdowns into breakthroughs.

"All problems contain the seeds of opportunity," Deepak Chopra writes.

It's just that we don't usually live there. When a sudden problem arises, an obstacle comes our way, or something blocks our path, we resist the obstacle. Our resistance keeps us stuck. What we resist resists us right back, in equal force. I once took lessons in Aikido and discovered that it is the fundamental principle in the martial arts.

"What you resist persists; what you can let be will let you be," Werner Erhard used to say.

So let us examine our current, and disempowering, relationship with breakdowns.

Breakdowns are stops, or interruptions, in the flow of action.

For example, one night I was driving home in the dark. Not only was it dark, but it was also raining heavily. I couldn't see very well, and I was aware of it. Still, I kept driving. I hit a curb hard. I said, "Oh, s . . . t!" to myself. I continued driving. In the next minute, I was crossing a bridge from the peninsula I had been on to my island. As I drove on the bridge, the noises underneath my right front tire grew louder and louder. The monsters of fear coursed through my body as the car became increasingly difficult to steer. There was nowhere to pull off. I had two roundabouts to navigate and a right turn to make before I could find a safe spot to stop and call for assistance.

The moment I hit the curb is the event that I call a breakdown: it is a stop in the flow of action. That sudden stop triggered a reaction. An expectation had been thwarted or violated (in this case, my assuming and hoping, as I could not see very well, that my drive home would be a normal one).

I invite you to recall a recent sudden breakdown *you* have had. Think of it first, before reading my next question. Put yourself in the place of the *very first* moment you realized you had a breakdown on your hands.

Got it?

Okay. What were the first two words you said to yourself in your head the moment you realized you had a breakdown?

Right. Probably the same as mine.

This reveals that our relationship to breakdowns is "oh, s . . . t." You could say that our approach to listening for breakdowns is that they are no good, and we should do our best to avoid them!

We live within a certain background story; a framework of interpretation or paradigm that suggests all problems are negative and good people do not encounter any. "Parents shouldn't have any problems. Leaders shouldn't have any problems. Good friends shouldn't have any problems. Spiritually aware people don't have any problems. I shouldn't have any problems."

Can you hear how debilitating that is? Because problems are part of our lives.

And so, we avoid them, deny them, minimize them, ignore them, and blame them, becoming victims of someone or something external to us. "It's not my fault!" we say, becoming victims.

The background context for all of this is, "There's something wrong here."

We live in a world of resistance and avoidance, and we attempt to solve our problems within that world—and it doesn't work.

Alfred D'Souza puts it this way:

> *For a long time, it had seemed to me that life was about to begin—real life. But there was always some obstacle in the way, something to be got through first, some unfinished business, time still to be served, a debt to be paid. Then life would begin. At last it dawned on me that these obstacles were my life.*

Maybe the next problem is simply your work showing up.

So, let us shift our thinking about the way we hold problems themselves, from the mindset that problems are bad and best avoided to a different mindset—a new structure of interpretation based on possibility.

What might be a powerful place to stand regarding obstacles?

Or, another way of asking this question is, "What are breakdowns an opportunity *for?*"

As you know from the last chapter, I stand for *breakdowns as an opportunity for transformation.* Inside that stand, I hold the perspective that whatever is given to me by the universe is a gift for my own evolution. My husband holds that same perspective.

When a teacher I was working with, a pragmatic philosopher named Arnold Siegel, learned that I had just been diagnosed with a brain tumor during Don's cancer struggle, he said to us upon entering his classroom, "What is with you two?"

Don immediately replied frankly, "We are on a very steep learning curve."

Perspective is huge. It saves the day. Your perspective gives you the world you are dancing in. Perspective creates an opening for a new sense of peace, access to creativity, and partnership with the universe.

To support you in carving out territory for inventing your own new perspective in this area, here is some profound wisdom from different traditions, including science, to empower your creative thinking as you take a stand for shifting your perspective about failures, obstacles, problems, and breakdowns.

A smooth sea never made a skillful mariner

Leaders learn by leading, and they learn best by leading in the face of obstacles. As weather shapes mountains, so problems make leaders.

Warren Bennis
On Becoming a Leader

The Chinese ideogram for crisis is also the same as the ideogram for opportunity.

> *Once you hold a crisis as an opportunity, every so-called upsetting situation will become an opportunity for the creation of something new and beautiful, and every so-called tormentor or tyrant will become your teacher. Reality is an interpretation. And if you choose to interpret reality in this way, you will have many teachers around you, and many opportunities to evolve.*
>
> Deepak Chopra
> *The Seven Spiritual Laws of Success*

> *All of life comes to us as a gift.*
>
> Brother David Steindl-Rast

> *In chemistry, Ilya Prigogine's prize-winning work also teaches a paradoxical truth, that disorder can be the source of new order. Prigogine coined the term "dissipative structures" for these newly discovered systems to describe their contradictory nature. Dissipation describes loss, a process of energy gradually ebbing away, while structure describes embodied order. Prigogine discovered that the dissipative activity of loss was necessary to create new order. Dissipation didn't lead to the death of a system. It was part of the process by which the system let go of its present form so that it could reorganize in a form better suited to the demands of its changed environment.*
>
> Meg Wheatley
> *Leadership and the New Science*

The Big Question

What is the most powerful stand you can take to have a life-giving relationship with obstacles and breakdowns that live for you like a living presence as you walk your path through life?

Here are some examples:

Breakdowns are openings for deepening my authenticity and integrity.

Breakdowns are opportunities for transformation.

Breakdowns are my teachers, opportunities for re-configuring the life I lead.

Breakdowns generate breakthroughs.

Breakdowns provide an opening for my deepest teachings.

Making This Your Own

Now, it's your turn to create a stand that is specific to facing breakdowns. What stand could you take that fosters an inspiring and enlivening relationship with breakdowns? What opportunities do breakdowns present for you?

Take some time with this; don't rush.

You might want to create a few stands. Write them down.

Which one most inspires you? The next time a breakdown hits you squarely, which one will be there for you, as a way of creating a powerful conversation?

When you feel satisfied, read it repeatedly, and maybe say it to yourself.

Stand for it. Live it. Inhabit the commitment of your own words.

When you have completed this, you will have cultivated a powerful relationship with breakdowns—one that opens you, through acceptance and surrender, to peace, power, and creativity instead of fear, resistance, and inaction.

You will have awakened yourself to your power to create life, to be bigger than the obstacle by it, rather than smaller and subsumed by it.

In the next chapter, we explore how managers and leaders have viewed breakdowns as opportunities, leading to extraordinary breakthroughs in real life.

Declaring Breakdowns as a Key to Breakthroughs

From Expectation to Commitment

The Challenge:

"It is time to close down the Santa Clara Tech Center."

It was June of 1988. Gary Egan, the general manager of the Bipolar Integrated Circuits Division of the Santa Clara Tech Center, had just been informed by the leadership of Hewlett-Packard that they would be shutting down. He was responsible for closing down the shop.

In Gary's own words, "The 180 people felt an incredible loss and anger over something they had worked very hard to preserve. These people were restricted to their jobs and not allowed to transfer. Orders for the product they produced doubled, yet we remained on a two-year closing schedule. We needed help and focused our energy on achieving more than four times the productivity the organization had achieved in the past period. We needed a dramatic change quickly."

They needed a wake-up call, a shake-up, a conversation so powerful that through it, they could shift who they were in the face of their outer circumstances, from resistance, being negative, bitter, and filled with blame, to people who could partner with Gary in closing down the business.

As Gary said, "We needed dramatic change quickly."

Gary had taken "The Heart of Leadership," a course I created and have been leading for forty years. The course allows for explosive breakthroughs in communication, integrity, listening, healing, and collaboration and partnership within organizations, shifting a culture from no trust to trust. In the public course Gary had taken, he learned that leaders could declare a breakdown, thereby rendering the status quo unacceptable.

The Action

Gary publicly declared a breakdown with his managers and asked me to lead an in-house course for his twenty senior managers. He knew what the course was, knew the conversation would produce a breakthrough, and knew it would get the job done.

Typically, people are graciously invited to the course and given an opportunity to accept or decline the invitation. This was an unusual situation. Gary told them all they had to be there.

When they walked in, it was clear they were unhappy. Many were displeased about taking the course itself. However, some were curious, eager to explore new territory for themselves, their leadership, their internal state of well-being and happiness, and their relationship with work.

One engineer stood out above the rest, making it clear he didn't want to be there. He was disgruntled, and the idea of making things work was far from his mind. He saw me as the enemy and spent the first two days sitting in the chair with his back to me.

Yes, I had some reactions going through me. I found it difficult at first to be with a participant who was sitting with his back to me.

The first breakdown I needed to handle was my own.

When we experience a breakdown, it means an expectation is operating in the background of something happening in the foreground.

What was the source of my reactions? What was that expectation?

Well, I expect people to come into doing work with me eager, interested in, if not committed to, their own breakthrough.

This guy was clearly not there.

When I looked to see what stand I could take, what new possibility I could declare, I stood for "Bill creates a breakthrough for himself in his relationship with the set of circumstances, this event, called a 'shut down.'" While he was very much in a deep, dark place, absolutely committed to unworkability, he would find his way to the light of day.

That stand opened the space for me to be with him exactly as he was being (and was not being) rather than resisting the way he was, which would have caused friction between us and upended the opportunity of the course.

I practiced the art of deep listening, listening *for* his commitment to ultimately make a difference and contribute to making the shutdown workable and an opportunity, *even though* all the evidence at the time was to the contrary.

On the third day of the course, I was pleasantly surprised and happy to see Bill sitting in his banquet chair, this time facing forward and looking at me. He seemed genuinely interested, and I could tell he was engaged.

The previous day, people had begun taking powerful stands in front of the room, advocating for a life filled with joy, passion, trust, and communication, both personally and in the workplace. The sweet scent of possibility lingered in the air. Perhaps he had forgiven the leaders of HP for declaring a shutdown; maybe he was starting to envision a life where he wouldn't have to suffer as much and feel so bitter; or perhaps he had begun to entertain new possibilities for himself.

Clearly, he had transported himself into new territory. He chose to be the first person to walk to the front of the room that day. Pausing, looking each person in the eye, he spoke, walked to the front of the room, and took a stand: "I declare this shutdown to be the most powerful and extraordinary shutdown HP has ever seen!"

I almost fell over, and so did everyone else. All the participants emerged from the course unified in a collaborative stand: "These next two years produce the most powerful shutdown HP has ever seen."

And it was. When the unit shut down two years later, in Gary's words, "Closure occurred within one month of the original twenty-four-month schedule, more than two times the original estimate of product was produced, and over 150 of the 180 employees involved accepted into new jobs at or above their previous pay level."

During that course, the team also stood for each individual's profound development, creating a workplace culture that would foster the realization of the "extraordinary shutdown."

The Ongoing Commitment to Development

During those two years, I worked with that team for one day a month and had conversations with individuals throughout that time. That one day was very potent. And how did I start each session? With one question:

"*What* is the most powerful breakdown you can declare this month?"

It was a compelling question that opened up a new realm of thinking. Once you declare a breakdown, you look at things differently, thinking "outside the box."

> *"The world we've made as a result of the level of thinking that we have done thus far creates problems that we cannot solve at the same level at which we created them."*
>
> Albert Einstein

They needed to think at a new level.

Each time we met:

1. They aligned on a breakdown to work on during the day. How did they align? Everyone presented the breakdown they

wanted to work on, and people asked questions. Through conversation, they reached a consensus on the most powerful breakdown to declare.

2. Then, together, they declared the breakdown and went to work. Once that particular breakdown was declared, the status quo for continuing with business as usual was no longer acceptable.

3. They examined the expectations that were living in the background and were the source of that breakdown. Each person looked for themselves.

4. Next, they committed to the future state by taking a stand. Examples: "All managers have been interviewed by prospective future managers by a specific date." Or "Our team has been hired by a certain date." Or "The x problem has been addressed."

5. They brainstormed and created new possibilities. For a conversation aimed at inventing new ideas to be effective, one needs to follow a rule: every idea is respected, whether you agree with it or not, and no idea is a bad idea. Creating a safe space frees people to generate ideas and explore possibilities without fear of criticism or being shot down. Comments like "That's a lousy idea," or "We did that before, and it didn't work," or "That will never work," or "Let me play devil's advocate" were not allowed during this brainstorming session. Those kinds of comments kill off possibility.

Sometimes, the ideas may sound silly or off-the-wall; you are brainstorming, after all, and letting your imagination run wherever it goes. I have frequently found that one idea leads to the next, and then the next, and suddenly, you have a breakthrough!

That frees everyone up. Here is an example.

This is the story an associate told me about working with the Air Force.

The US Air Force operates a base in the Cascade Mountains. In fall and spring, ice storms cause problems for utilities. They deposit significant amounts of ice on the power transmission lines, and if it accumulates, it overstresses and snaps the power lines. So, they had to clear the ice.

Clearing the ice was perilous for the linemen. They would ascend icy towers and shake the lines with long, hooked poles. They hated the job, which involved lengthy treks through the woods at risky heights and in uncomfortable conditions. Several personnel fell and sustained injuries. It was costly on many levels.

They held a brainstorming session with line supervisors, secretaries, accountants, and mail room clerks. My consultant friend announced the rules of the engagement and said, "No idea is a bad idea." Someone volunteered to be the scribe and write down what everybody said.

Over the break, my friend overheard someone talking to someone else. "I hate this job. Last week, I was chased by a bear. I could have been seriously hurt."

When the meeting resumed, my colleague recounted what she had overheard on behalf of everyone having a stake in the conversation. The first voice said, "Why don't we just train the bears to climb the poles? Perhaps they'd shake the poles enough to knock the ice off."

Although it was intended as a joke, Linda told the scribe, "Write that down!" She took the suggestion seriously.

The second voice spoke: "The real problem is getting the bears to climb the poles sequentially."

Linda said, "Write that down."

The third voice added, "Well, we have to make the climb worth the bears' efforts. Let's put honey pots on top of the poles."

Linda responded, "Write that down."

At this point, her inner critic kicked in, and she started thinking maybe it was not such a great idea to share the story about the comment she had overheard.

A sarcastic lineman spoke next. "How about expropriating the helicopters the generals fly around in? We could use them to put honey pots on top of the poles after an ice storm."

There was a long silence. Suddenly, a secretary spoke. She said, "You know, I was a nurse's aide in Vietnam. Injured soldiers were flown from the field hospitals by helicopters, and the downwash from the blades was amazing. What if the helicopters flew over the lines at a low altitude? Would the downwash from the blades be powerful enough to knock the ice off?"

There was no laughter in that room. Only a stunned silence. It was a breakthrough. And today, after ice storms, you can hear helicopters flying over the power lines to clear them. The HP managers held similar potent conversations for possibility.

After the conversations for possibilities, they grounded the best ideas, making them doable and feasible. They asked each other what it was time for, planned out their project from the future, envisioned themselves in the future, with their commitment already having been fulfilled, and planned from the future. They looked at possible requests they could make for resources and to whom, and made requests and promises to each other for actions they would take. They spent the rest of the month making requests of others and being in action. By the following month, the breakthrough of that particular breakdown had occurred.

The following month, they'd declare the next breakdown.

Gary says, "We were able to convert possibilities into firm action plans. The work moved people beyond what is bad about this to what opportunities this experience gives me."

In two years, the plant shut down. The VP of Hewlett-Packard called it the most extraordinary shutdown HP had ever seen.

Paving the Way for Declaring Breakdowns

Since declaring breakdowns is so powerful, one would think we would do so all the time. But we don't. What stops us?

Often, it's just plain that we want to look good, and we don't see being visible about our failures or obstacles as an opportunity.

We are especially unwilling to declare problems when we don't know the solution or how to take effective action. We think we need to have the answer before we can begin, rather than allowing and trusting the conversation to reveal appropriate and effective action.

The personnel manager of the Santa Clara Tech Center had a problem with the staff being interviewed by managers from other sites for future jobs. She said, "There's nothing we can do, it's just too far away."

But, once she declared a breakdown within the group, new possibilities for designing conversations over the year out, through other managers getting involved and making connections with people they knew in other sites, the whole knot untied itself.

I worked with HP's Inkjet Business Unit for fifteen years. I led advanced and introductory courses for all their engineers and consulted the executive team. After Gary retired, Greg Merten, to whom Gary had passed the torch, became the general manager. You may remember the story about Diane Merten and their son, Scott. They are the same family.

Greg Merten and I worked closely together for many years, along with Mickey Connolly, another consultant, whom I had introduced into HP. We met regularly with Greg's senior team, spending a full day together approximately once a month, much as I had with Gary's team in Santa Clara

Looking back on that period, Greg once told me that the real value of our work together was not a particular methodology, but the depth and quality of dialogue the team learned to sustain. Instead of defaulting to debate, defensiveness, or the need to be right, they learned to slow down, stay engaged with differing perspectives, and genuinely listen to one another. Over time, that shift allowed new thinking to emerge—thinking that no one person could have generated alone.

Greg would often reflect and share with others that the breakthroughs they achieved through this way of working translated into extraordinary business results, contributing hundreds of millions of dollars in incremental value to HP's bottom line.

You can see how mastering the art of sacred listening mightily contributes to both results and accomplishment in the world.

One day, during one of our monthly meetings, Keith, a member of Greg's team, arrived late. He was a tall, healthy, strong man with brown hair and a calm, steady disposition. Keith was a mentor to many people in his organization. Keith was clearly flustered and apologized for being late. This was unusual.

After greeting him, the others asked him, "What happened?" or "Is there anything wrong?"

He said, "No."

One issue that had plagued the team for approximately six months involved a problem with one of the pens, code-named "Monet." Failing to resolve this issue was costing the Ink Jet Business Unit a significant amount of money.

Keith oversaw Monet.

During the meeting, Keith kept leaving to make phone calls in the next room. He did this about four times. Each time, people asked him if he wanted to share anything about what was going on with him. He said, "No." While his body was in the room, he was clearly distracted and not focused on what the others were working on.

At one point, again leaving the meeting, he returned, striding purposefully into the room. There was clearly a different energy about him, a sense of purposeful intention. He stood tall. He stood straight. He was like an animal that would not let go of whatever was in its grip.

He picked up one of the chairs, asked Greg to turn around, put his chair across from him, looked him in the eye, and said, *"I'm declaring a breakdown."*

Everything stopped. His declaration altered the conversation in that room, and everyone was relieved. It had been a six-month problem. With that declaration, the problem with Monet became unacceptable and intolerable. It was time for a breakthrough.

Stand-taking renders the status quo unacceptable.

We began a new conversation about creating new possibilities; possibilities not yet invented or seen. They had to give up their old way of thinking.

Up until that moment, the way they structured the organization's work for pens was through silos. Each team worked on a particular pen. That day, they broke out of their own paradigm of working in silos, turning toward each other and asking for global resources.

Their brilliant idea was: "Who are our best chemists from all of our sites around the world? Let's put them in a room together, give them food, and tell them not to come out until they solve the problem."

And that's exactly what they did.

In two days, those chemists solved the problem.

About fifteen years ago, I was leading a course in the region where we provide our public courses. There was an HP man in the course. When I told that story to the attendees, Suraj jumped out of his seat and said excitedly, "I was one of those chemists!!!" He was so proud and felt so acknowledged.

Making This Your Own

What is a breakdown you could declare?

Think about that, ruminate about that. You may have several ideas. Then, pick one that inspires you, and say, "I am declaring a breakdown!" And then get to work.

Name the expectation or the commitment that's been thwarted.

Ask yourself what new stand you could take, or what commitment you could declare? That new stand becomes the foundation for your breakthrough in the area.

Now, engage in a wide-open conversation about possibilities for fulfilling that stand, including "outside the nine dots ideas." For example: "Let's move from silo to global group." Or "I can go wherever I need to go to have my surgery performed by the best surgeon I can find."

Go to work on grounding your idea, making it doable and feasible. For example: "Let's put the chemists in one room and tell them not to come out until it is resolved," and "Who are those chemists?" Brainstorm until it becomes clear.

As soon as you hear, "Oh, okay, this is doable!" move into action by making requests and/or promises.

For example: "I ask you, Suraj, to get yourself on a plane by Wednesday and show up in Corvallis on Thursday morning."

Once you are in action, inside your commitment, the power of intent comes into play. You'll have to test this one out in life, but you will see that *Providence moves too. All sorts of things occur that would not otherwise have occurred,* W. H. Murray.

Don't take a puny stand. Take a great stand; one that is larger than yourself. One that lights up your life, that inspires you, that brings you to life. One that brings into being, brings into existence, a breakthrough that is worthy of the power and the greatness that you are, that everyone is. Then, watch and let the universe move on your behalf.

CHAPTER 22

Getting Interested in Getting Interested

Honoring Others

It was baseball season, April had arrived, and I lost my husband to baseball.

My husband is generally totally supportive. I mean, if they made a French perfume out of the essence of Don, it would be called "Parfum du Support."

But baseball season is another matter. Once the baseball season starts—football, too, but baseball, he devotes more frequent time to—nobody messes with that.

So, here I was almost every night, moaning and groaning, miserable, suffering, making my husband wrong, and generally being a "clod of ailments and grievances, complaining that the world would not devote itself to making (me) happy," to quote George Bernard Shaw.

What was my internal dialogue? *He doesn't care about me. He doesn't support me. If he really loved me, he wouldn't be watching baseball all the time.*

And then, I woke up.

I realized I was running a number in my head, and not an empowering one at that, making myself miserable. I saw that if I wanted to enjoy Don's companionship during this time of year, I'd better get interested in baseball.

That would be better than being annoyed all the time.

Except I wasn't interested in baseball.

Okay, I said to myself, *well, at the very least, what you can do is get interested in getting interested in baseball.*

There is a principle in development *that when someone really needs to go into development to create a new reality for themselves or break themselves up on behalf of a larger possibility, they first have to get interested in doing so. If they are not interested, they have to get interested in getting interested.*

I knew this. I teach this. I am committed to living what I teach.

So, I looked at how I could get interested. I thought about it. *I know,* I said to myself. *I could have Don take me to a game—and see what, about the game, I could get interested in!*

"Let's go to a baseball game," I said to Don.

"WHAT?????" He practically screamed in my ear.

And go to a game we did.

Fortunately, the year was 1995. We live on an island across from Seattle, and the Mariners had an amazing team: Randy Johnson, Ken Griffey, Alex Rodriguez, Edgar Martinez, and Dan Wilson—a star-studded cast.

It was the perfect year to get interested in baseball.

Before we left home that day, I made one commitment to myself: I would enjoy myself. I would do nothing that wasn't enjoyable. I was committed to having fun.

The day of the game was warm and beautiful. The first thing I saw after they took our tickets was a hot dog stand. I love hot dogs, and they had New York dogs too. So, I bought a hot dog and piled it high with mustard, sauerkraut, and onions. Yum! I was happy.

A little later, on the way to our seats, I saw a beer stand, so I bought myself some beer. Now I had both beer and a hot dog. What could be better?

Our seats were pretty darn good. They were about twenty rows up, a little to the right of the third baseline. The day was sunny, and there were lots and lots of people around. In fact, that day, the stadium was filled to capacity with 50,000 fans.

A short while after I started enjoying my hot dog, I noticed a woman near me stand up and put her right hand high into the air. Meanwhile, people in the whole row were passing money towards a man who had his hand behind his back, and from the hand behind his back, he threw something into this woman's raised right arm. I was so surprised! I asked Don, "What's that about?"

He said, "Oh, that man is selling peanuts that are wrapped in aluminum foil." I was blown away.

I asked Don if I could do the same thing, though I never believed I would ever be able to catch the peanuts. He said, "Sure."

I stood up, and we started passing the money down, and oh my god. Those peanuts landed right in my palm. I couldn't believe it!

And I love peanuts. So, there I was, quite happy, eating my hot dog with sauerkraut, drinking my beer, and eating peanuts. I threw the shells on the ground. It seemed to be part of the culture.

All of a sudden, everyone stood up. Don told me to stand. "Why?" I asked.

"Because we are going to sing the 'Star-Spangled Banner.'"

Now, considering myself somewhat of an ex-hippie non-conformist, I was a bit resistant to this. Nevertheless, I reluctantly stood up, like everyone else. Then I started singing with everyone else. Like everyone else, I found my hand on my heart. Like everyone else, I found myself in a community. And like everyone else, I began to realize how much I appreciate living in America.

In that one moment, I felt a new sense of belonging, belonging to a community. I shifted from being separate from the world to being connected to each and every human being in that stadium. We were One.

Tears rolled down my cheek.

My heart swelled.

"Okay," I said to Don. "We can go home now."

Don said, "The game hasn't started."

We stayed.

I found it fascinating. There was this young man, Alex, who kept "sneaking" off first base each time he arrived at first base. Don told me that what Alex was doing was called "stealing."

I started getting the jargon. I entered the world of "Baseball Speak."

I thought it was so sweet each time a runner reached first or third base, the way the men were bonding with one another, particularly with the pat on the "*tuchus*," a good Jewish word for "rear end." Don told me about the first and third base coaches and what they were there for.

Don talked to me throughout the game. He pointed out the positioning of players, or why the shortstop got so close in at a certain point, how we could tell a bunt was coming, why a pitcher intentionally walked a player, and how the pitcher and catcher communicated. That day, as I gained new insight into the language of baseball, I entered that world. I entered Don's world. And I expanded my own.

The following week, I was leading a course in Corvallis. Don was at home. That Wednesday night, there was a game. Back in my hotel room, I watched the game. Of course! During the second inning, Griffey hit a homer. I called Don on the phone and said, "How about that homer Griffey just hit?"

In total surprise, he yelled, "WHAT? You're watching the game?"

I no longer have any upsets whenever baseball season arrives at our relationship's doorstep. After all, I get to enjoy life with my husband.

Making This Your Own

What source of dissatisfaction in your life would you like to transform into a source of acceptance, if not joy?

What could you get interested in getting interested in?

What new actions could you take to create greater joy and connection with someone in your life?

Prepare to be amazed by what opens up for you out of those new actions.

CHAPTER 23

Bringing Gratefulness, Faith, and Stand-Taking to a Crisis

Making the Impossible Possible

Sometimes, life hits us over the head with a crisis that seems so powerful, so difficult, and so impossible to handle that we lose heart, over and over and over again. And during those times, it is incumbent upon us to bring to bear, to call forth possibility in the face of no possibility, over and over and over again.

Such was the case with my husband when, in February of 1999, Don was examined and was told by his doctors, "You have a stage four lymphoma."

We were frightened and blind to Possibility. We could barely think or see. Our daughter was one and a half years old.

The first action we knew we needed to take was to attend a cancer retreat that could open new doors of thinking and perception. We knew that creating a transformational shift, some peace, and some room to breathe spaciously was critical to our journey through this time. We called Commonweal, a cancer healing center in Bolinas, California, which was full for six months. They told us about Harmony Hill Cancer Retreat Center on Hood Canal, within an hour of our home.

The retreat fulfilled its purpose. The other individuals alongside us shared our difficulty. We were all afraid of death.

A wise and compassionate leader guided us through beautiful, profound conversations. These conversations provided us with a boat to sail from the island of resistance to death to the island of acceptance, allowing death to become a constant companion in our lives.

Being at peace with death opened a new door, a door to possibility, through which Don could hear an inner voice of spirit calling to him—a voice of vitality, whose root word is "life," and courage, whose root word is "heart." The presence of both Vitality and Courage accompanied us on our learning-filled path.

The first invasive treatment, an eight-month course of chemotherapy, began.

Worry and fear, twin brothers, accompanied us on the path, and we worked inwardly to allow them as human emotions, even opening our hearts to them—or "inviting them in," as Rumi instructs us to do in his poem "The Guest House." Once invited in, they lost some of their power to debilitate us, as we stopped resisting them.

Within two months after the chemotherapy, we discovered that the treatment plan had not worked. The tumors returned.

We were devastated. At first, we could not move or think. We both went inward, attending to our internal state, releasing disappointment, being present with what was, and letting go of our attachment to a successful outcome. Once we received the situation for what it was, we could begin to respond creatively, inventing new possibilities for different paths forward.

Once we allowed the situation to be what it was, Don discovered an alternative treatment in San Diego to consider. While he ultimately decided not to pursue it, the doctor there shared something crucial with him. Don asked, "What would you do in my case?"

The doctor paused, thought, and said, "You know, Don? We have found that those who do best are those who have given it up to God."

In that still moment, something inside both of us exhaled.

Don embraced that. What had been said was so meaningful that faith led the way through the rest of the journey. You could think of it as a profound trust in the unfolding, whatever the outcome: a surrender, a letting go of will and force, and of the illusion that we have control.

By now in this book, you have heard me speak often of taking a stand. In the crucible of Don's illness, that distinction became deeply personal and real.

A stand is not stubbornness.

A stand is not willpower.

A stand is not a solitary act taken against something

A stand is not a tactic to force the universe into doing what we want.

A stand is something very different.

A stand is a way of aligning yourself with the most profound truth within you. It is a commitment born from the heart, not one made through effort or force. It is a commitment to live inside a created possibility, including when there is no evidence that that possibility will ever be actualized.

A stand is more like a quality of surrender. Not the surrender of defeat, but the surrender that opens the door to partnership.

Partnership with what?

With life itself.

With your own inner wisdom

With the Divine, however you name the Mystery that accompanies you.

A stand is a declaration of who you are, regardless of circumstances. It is an opening to possibility, an invitation to collaborate with a Spirit greater than your own will. It is a way of saying, quietly and clearly, "I am committed to having my life shaped by this commitment."

In this way, a stand becomes a place to stand on a ground that supports you, a compass that orients you, a conversation that lifts you out of resignation and into the domain of the possible.

When Don and I encountered the limits of what medicine could offer, it was his stand for Life that carried us forward. It opened a space where new paths could appear. It created room for grace, synchronicity, and the quiet guidance of the universe to make itself known, as we stood in faith, trusting in the unfolding.

The Sufis say, "Trust in God, but tie your camel first."

Don tied every camel he had. Throughout his journey, he had an integrative oncologist with him. He also received acupuncture once a week, psychotherapy to address residual emotional baggage, massages once a month, and a change in diet.

After the first chemotherapy, he underwent two rounds of high-dose chemotherapy to determine his eligibility for a stem cell transplant. He spent a month in the hospital navigating that process. The procedure involved recirculating his blood to harvest stem cells. It was a risky endeavor, as Don was without an immune system for some time. When the stem cells were reintroduced to his bloodstream, Don remarked that he could feel them dancing like angels in his veins.

Two months later, the tumors returned.

The oncologists were done; they had done everything they knew to do.

Serendipitously, Don had received a gift several months earlier. While preparing for one treatment or another, a nurse had told Don about a brand-new treatment called a monoclonal antibody that her husband had used that worked for him.

Once again, Don stood for possibility. He persuaded his physicians to start him on a course of Rituxan.

It worked. It set his tumors back for a year. Then, he did a second course. It worked, too, setting them back for nine months. Then, he did a third course. The tumors returned in six months. "The shine has gone off the silver bullet," Don said.

And it was time to move on.

That was the end of the line for the doctors. "Go home and pack your bags," they said.

For many—perhaps you, or someone you love—this is the moment when the journey turns inward: a time to create a new space; a space for love, for joy, for being fully alive while alive; for leaving others with completion and peace; for teaching, for giving, for serving; for being fully present while giving what you have to give; for approaching death as the next new beginning.

Don and I flew to Hawaii to shift our environment; to slow down, reflect, contemplate, and listen deeply for what was next. We came to be present to what was so, without resistance. We surrendered.

And a quiet voice, a voice of remembrance, revelation, and insight, whispered: "We live in conversation."

The conversations we live in affect us. They are not nothing. They are everything. And we were living in a conversation of, "It's all over, go home and die." We said to one another, "There is someone out there who inhabits a different conversation, someone for whom the possibility of life still exists. We have to find that person."

We came home committed to finding someone who was part of that conversation, dedicated to entering a new world of possibilities. Within a week, a naturopath we knew referred us to another physician experienced in treating cancer patients. When Don called him, the physician mentioned a treatment program that had worked for others and might work for Don as well.

I do not know if this treatment would work for you or anyone you love. All I know is that it worked for Don.

Don began the treatment—fifty grams of high-dose intravenous vitamin C two times a week. After six weeks, the tumors were gone, and the blood tests were normal.

Eight weeks later, with everything still appearing normal, Don said, "Okay. That's good. I'm going to double down on this. I am going to do the whole thing again."

He did.

The tumors stayed gone.

Then, a month later, he repeated the entire treatment.

And that was that.

Since 2004, we have not seen cancer again.

Making This Your Own

As I reflect on that time in our lives now, what stands out most is not the sequence of events, or the treatments, or even the miracle of Don's recovery. What stands out is the way a stand can transform the very atmosphere of a life. A stand shifts the inner landscape long before anything changes on the outside. It alters the conversation you live inside, changes the questions you ask, and opens the door to guidance you could not have heard before. And so it becomes natural—almost inevitable—to turn toward your own life and ask: Where is a stand being called for in me?

Often, we remain in the realm of wishing, wanting, or hoping rather than standing for something. The two are very different.

Wishing is passive.

Wanting is tentative.

Hoping keeps us in waiting.

A stand is lived. It is embodied. It is a commitment you inhabit.

A stand is not taken for the sake of controlling an outcome. A stand is taken for the sake of who you choose to be in the face of whatever life brings. It is a way of aligning yourself with a possibility that calls to you, or a vision that is larger than yourself, even if there is no evidence for it yet.

So, I invite you to consider:

What stand could you take that would create a new and life-giving space of possibility for yourself, for humanity, for the Earth, for the future of mankind?

Where could you bring gratefulness in the very midst of difficulty?

Where, in your own life, could you trust the universe so profoundly that you relax your grip on steering the outcome, and instead become present to guidance, synchronicity, and grace?

What emotions might you include, allow, or welcome rather than resist or deny?

I remind you again of the beginning of W.H. Murray's quote, because it bears repeating:

> *Until one is committed there is hesitancy, the chance to draw back, always ineffectiveness. Concerning all acts of initiative (and creation), there is one elementary truth, the ignorance of which kills countless ideas and splendid plans: that the moment one definitely commits oneself, then Providence moves too.*

And remember: one never knows what form "Providence" will take. Life rarely resembles the pictures we have in our minds of how things "should" look. That is how faith and taking a stand become a steadying force—an anchor that returns us to peace.

Your work is not to choreograph the universe. Your work is to remain true to the possibility you stand for, to return to your own heart, and to observe with curiosity—and even wonder—how life unfolds in response.

When you take an authentic stand—one born of your heart—you awaken the power of intent. An energetic resonance is created, a magnetic field that invites new possibilities, new ideas, new openings, and new conversations that could not have appeared otherwise.

So I invite you to experiment with this. Take it into your life. Try it on gently, as you might try on a garment to see how it fits and feels. Wear it for a while. Notice what opens.

What stand can you take—or are you called to take—in the face of circumstances that seem immovable?

Where is faith calling you?

> *Faith is the courageous confidence that trusts in the source of all gifts.*
> — Brother David Steindl-Rast

Can you trust the universe so much that you are willing to give up being in control—and at the same time stand wholeheartedly for a possibility that brings you alive?

As you explore this territory, be gentle with yourself. A stand is not something you force. It is something you grow into, something that reveals itself as you listen deeply. When it comes, you will know. It will carry a quiet rightness, a clarity, and a sense of alignment with who you most truly are. And as you walk within that commitment, step by step, the world around you begins to reorganize itself in response. Life meets you where you stand.

Stand-taking opens us to partnership with life. Faith opens us to collaboration with the Mystery. And together, they prepare the ground for a deeper listening—the listening that arises when we surrender to what is, soften into presence, and invite the sacred to meet us.

It is to that listening that we now turn.

PART IV
Awakening Your Sacred Listening for Spirit

When you surrender to what is and so become fully present, the past ceases to have any power. The realm of Being, which had been obscured by the mind, then opens up. Suddenly, a great stillness arises within you, an unfathomable sense of peace.
And within that peace, there is great joy.
And within that joy, there is love.
And at the innermost core, there is the sacred, the immeasurable.
That which cannot be named.
Eckhart Tolle, *Practicing the Power of Now*

CHAPTER 24

Finding my Thread

From Angst to Trusting Myself

Between 1972 and 1974, as I started my journey into spirituality and personal development (which means the same thing to me), I also began the journey of discovering purpose in life.

When you begin to uncover, unravel, unseal, and reveal the purpose of your life and who you are as a unique being meant to accomplish that purpose, it becomes a beacon— a torch that illuminates your path, much like the North Star that guides and shines a light on your journey. Life becomes much simpler when you "follow your own thread," as William Stafford says in his beautiful poem:

> *The Way It Is*
> *There's a thread that you follow. It goes among*
> *things that change. But it doesn't change.*
> *People wonder about what you are pursuing.*
> *You have to explain about the thread . . .*

"You don't ever let go of the thread," William Stafford says at the end of his poem.

In this chapter, I share with you the extraordinary story of when I first began to find my thread.

In the next chapter, I intend to leave you with a clear map and some resourceful questions to support you in navigating your way to your own thread.

My personal story of discovering a new aspect of my unique work on the planet started from a conversation with an Indian man, Baba Muktananda, who was well-known in India as a guru. I first "met" Baba in 1972 through his photographs. Two years later, I met him in person. During an extraordinary conversation I had with him at that time, I was both 1) freed to pursue my own path in my own way, and 2) given my new name, which gave me further clarity about following my own path in my own way. I stepped into my new life, and I have been shaping that life ever since.

The time? November 1972. So, we go back to the very beginning of my quest and an experience that came my way one month before the breakthrough I made with my father, which I shared with you in Chapter One.

It was an occasion in which I lost my mind and found my heart.

I was taking a course called Silva Mind Control, held in the leader's beautiful Craftsman home in Piedmont, California. I sat in a chair in a living room with dark mahogany walls alongside several other people. It was a restful space. Photos of a strange-looking Indian man in orange robes adorned the walls and shelves—photos that aroused my curiosity, but I chose to ignore them. I was there to learn to control my mind. As you may recall, my first husband and I were going through a divorce at the time.

Where I had been clear before, I now felt uncertain about the direction of my life and found myself grappling with the profound question, "Who am I, anyway?"

I realized that I had intertwined my identity with my roles in life—as a teacher, daughter, wife, and the "good girl" always striving to please. Furthermore, my mind and inner dialogue were quite noisy: *What am I going to do next? Should I take a break from teaching? How will I discover who I truly am?*

What will the future bring? What should I do with my life now? I needed to create some distance from my incessant "radio nonstop thinking," as Thich Nhat Hanh refers to the chatter of what Buddhists call "the monkey mind." That was the basis for my decision to enroll in this course.

While the course I attended was good, an unusual event happened that was even more striking.

In the afternoon of the first day, as I listened to the course instructor distinguish something about the mind, waves of heat, somewhat like electric energy, poured from above into the crown of my head and permeated my entire body. Wave after wave of warmth, bliss, and Life filled my whole being.

I didn't know what was happening. I didn't understand it. I just let it happen. After all, it was all I could do. It wasn't stoppable by thinking. Ignoring it didn't work either. I just had to experience it, to be with it, and move with it.

That surprising experience of heat and energy shook me to my core. I was not frightened, even though I didn't understand what was happening or what it meant. I simply allowed it to be what it was, fully experiencing it. I later learned that many others had similar experiences in the presence of the man in the orange robes. On that path, such an experience is not unusual and is referred to as "the transmission of Shakti," or divine energy.

The deepest, strongest, most potent, Life-giving aspect of that passage was the profound experience of being loved. I "knew" that I was loved in the depths of my being.

Something had settled.

I was at peace.

I belonged.

As I left this beautiful, energy-filled home to step back into the world of time and "normality," onto the wide, oak-tree-lined street, I shared my experience with the course teacher.

"Ah," she said. "You've met Baba. Now, you have to go to India."

And go to India I did, more than once. But not before I met Baba in person, in a small, yellow house in Aspen, Colorado.

Baba Muktananda, whose name means "the bliss of freedom," had come into Werner Erhard's life through Raz Ingrasci, who encouraged Werner to meet Baba in India. Werner later invited Baba to visit the United States and to come to the centers where est graduate seminars and trainings were being offered so that graduates could have the opportunity to meet him.

I was living in Colorado at the time. During that year, I had taken the forty-day Arica training, participated fully in the *est* graduate seminars, read Muktananda's books, and begun a meditation practice according to his instructions. I was very happy doing all that work.

I moved to Boulder in January, where I lived in a house with other Arica students and trainers, diving deep into the teachings of Oscar Ichazo, the founder of the Arica School. This was an eclectic blend of Buddhism, Western psychology, Zen, the Enneagram, African dance, and Body/Mind work. The following summer, Baba arrived in Aspen.

When Baba came to that yellow house in Aspen, I had the extraordinary opportunity to spend two weeks with Baba Muktananda each morning. Every day, he held a session he called "*darshan,*" which means being in the presence of a holy man or saint.

He wore a red or orange sari every day and had a short beard and mustache. Standing five foot six and slim of build, his inner smile of pure bliss radiated from his Indian face, mainly through his deep brown eyes. He also displayed a red dot, called a "*bindi,*" right between his eyebrows. A Hindu custom, the *bindi* ornamentally symbolizes the third eye, the seat of wisdom.

Though Baba later had hundreds of thousands of devotees and was widely known around the world, at the time, only about two to eight of us were blessed to have the intimate experience of "*darshan,*" during which we simply sat with him, meditated with him, chanted with him, or talked with him.

The experience of being with him was extraordinary. I had a deep, authentic, and abiding sense of being loved—not by another human being, but simply loved. I was loved by the universe, fully accepted, fully known, and fully embraced, just as I was, with all my successes, failures, and quirks. I felt as if the entirety of my life—the past, the present, and the future—was being accepted, embraced, and simply okay. I was at peace.

Baba would say, at the end of every talk, "God dwells within you as you."

Baba opened my heart to myself.

While I was so happy to be there with Baba, I had a big issue. I knew I needed to talk with him about it, as it was strangling me. My heart was heavy. Devoted to following the path of freedom, development, and spiritual growth, my heart was tied up in a proverbial knot. There was a big question that I wanted to pose to Baba. I knew he could direct me rightly.

On the third day I spent with him that week, during *darshan*, I approached him. My heart pounded in my throat, and I was trembling; I somehow knew this would be a turning point in my journey. I said, pleading: "Baba! I don't know what to do with my life from here. There are three paths before me. I did the *est* training, and I love that body of work. I know I could be a leader there, and I want to immerse myself in it. I'm already two years into deep work with the Arica School, learning about how all the paths lead to the same place. Now that I've met you in person, I just want to follow you everywhere and anywhere! What should I do?"

I waited, my entire being depending on what he would say next.

Baba laughed. And laughed and laughed and laughed.

And then he hit me with his peacock feathers. He always had peacock feathers with him; in India, the peacock is considered a holy bird because it eats garbage and turns it into beauty.

The peacock feathers tickled me. He waved them back and forth across my face, grazing my face, as he laughed and laughed.

Then he became serious. He looked penetratingly into my eyes, his gaze intense and pointed.

And he said, "Do whatever makes you happy."

That was exactly what my heart needed to hear.

Another full stop moment.

The whole Earth moved inside of me. I began weeping, and my entire body relaxed. I was deeply moved by a combination of joy, gratitude, relief, and the sudden realization that I was awake enough to trust myself, trust my intuition, and follow my heart. It was an extraordinary recognition.

And I have continued to do so ever since. The universe has always looked out for me, as long as I followed my heart. When I didn't—when I followed my head instead, or someone else's good advice for my life—I ran into trouble and became unhappy. That's how I found out that I needed to make course corrections again and again.

A few days later, his next one-on-one conversation with me further opened the door to connecting with "my thread" as I stepped into my purpose.

Throughout the week, as people visited him, Baba gave them Hindu names. I realized I wanted Baba to name me because I didn't like the nickname I had been using since I was thirteen. Each morning, I started meditating, asking Baba to give me "the right name." I didn't want a name that was too unusual; many Hindu names sounded long and somewhat strange to the English-speaking ear. I knew I wanted to offer "work in the world" to be of service, and I wanted my name to be one that I could use professionally.

One morning, after my meditation, I somehow knew that that day was the day to ask Baba for a name.

When I walked into the living room of the house that day, Baba was already sitting in his chair. I took one step forward toward where he was seated to ask for a name, but Baba stopped me with a gesture. He fluidly moved his hand from above his head to his lap, and as he made that gesture, he said the word, "Amba."

I stopped. I had no idea what was happening or what he was saying to me.

Then, he said, "Mickie, Mickie, Mickie, Mickie, Mickie" (which was my nickname), and then, "I can't remember that name." (Which was very funny, as he had just said it five times.)

"Your name is Amba. Come, come, sit. Let me tell you the story of Amba."

I sat in front of him.

Baba began: "Once upon a time, there was an evil demon in the kingdom of heaven. He was so powerful and so evil that none of the gods, by themselves, could slay him. So they called a conclave, gathered together, and discussed the matter. Out of that conversation, they decided to create a goddess and imbue her with each of their powers. Then she could slay the evil demon. And they did. And she did.

"And the kingdom of heaven became once more a peaceful place."

Hearing that story, I sensed that Baba was letting me know my path was eclectic; that it was my purpose in life, my calling, my thread, and my way to embody the teachings from as many paths as possible that "made me happy," paths that attracted me and called to me.

I would fulfill my life's purpose by leading a full and meaningful life, allowing life to flow through me, sharing my learnings, teachings, and discoveries through wholehearted living with others, and expressing this in my own voice and in my own way.

Living that, being that, and contributing that would allow for an awakening of my awareness, an awakening of my heart, an opening into my loving myself, restoring a condition of trust in myself and others, and allowing life's obstacles to serve as a gift to the spirit, to my own evolution.

In that way, I could be of service to the world.

And that speaks to me of living a life well-lived.

Amba was the perfect name. It was my calling, my path, and my truth.

And now, in the next chapter, we turn to you. We create a space for you to begin discovering your own calling, your unique path, and your purpose in life—that place within you where you can live from your true joy through listening for the Sacred.

CHAPTER 25

Leading a Life of True Joy

From Separateness to Belonging

When you have fully accepted and embraced what is, as well as what is not, you enter a new land: a land of wholeness, presence, centeredness, and peace.

So, we begin the final two chapters of our book. Many of the distinctions are easy to express, yet I recognize that embodying them can sometimes require deep practice; for example, accepting others as they are and as they are not, and accepting life as it is and as it is not.

It takes commitment, creativity, and discipline to dedicate time and give yourself the space to let go—to release the expectations, judgments, and standards in your mind, to silence the voices that insist life should be different, and to simply be with what is as a gift from the universe. As Eckhart Tolle adds, "with that peace, there is great joy. And within that joy, there is love."

In these final chapters, my intention is for you to explore new paths to joy, love, and service as you deepen your ability to listen for the sacred. We will open pathways for you to discover your own purpose and also create completion, appreciation, and acknowledgment for the work you've done in your life while reading this book. We will also examine what it takes to design a future worth living.

You will discover your own path, as I did. The journey always begins by letting go of who you are not, and connecting with your own authenticity, your own wholeness.

Here, you can open yourself to unconditional love.

Here you can create connection from disconnection.

Here you can receive life as a gift.

Here, you can be still enough to allow your own greater intelligence to guide you in becoming the author or the artist of your life.

It starts with prioritizing yourself in your life. This is not selfish; it is the essence of Self-Care. "We teach who we are," as Parker Palmer says, and "anytime we can listen to true self, and give it the care it requires, we do so not only for ourselves, but for the many others whose lives we touch."

Many years ago, I came across a quote by George Bernard Shaw that was so rich, meaningful, life-affirming, and enlightening that I want to end my book with it, taking you on a deep dive into the pure, profound, and powerful waters Shaw offers us.

May the spirit of his words awaken your heart and fill you with the possibility of embracing Spirit, embracing Purpose, and embracing Life.

A Splendid Torch

This is the true joy in life, the being used for a purpose recognized by yourself as a mighty one . . . the being a force of nature instead of a feverish, selfish little clod of ailments and grievances complaining that the world will not devote itself to making you happy.

I am of the opinion that my life belongs to the whole community, and as long as I live, it is my privilege to do for it whatever I can. I want to be thoroughly used up when I die, for the harder I work, the more I live. I rejoice in life for its own sake. Life is no "brief candle" to me. It is a sort of splendid torch which I have got hold of for the moment, and I want to make it burn as brightly as possible before handing it on to future generations.

–George Bernard Shaw[1]

I have lived with this quote by George Bernard Shaw, the great Irish playwright, for years.

These sentiments have stirred my heart, my spirit, and my life. These two paragraphs have become a sort of mantra for me, a *leitmotif*—a phrase that recurs repeatedly, subtly changing each time—whose essence has remained constant throughout my life.

George Bernard Shaw's words gave birth to a whole raft of inquiry questions that have guided my life; questions I have intentionally continued to live with and which have lit up my life. Planting those questions, like seeds in fertile soil, has served as humus, allowing a loving life to sprout, be nourished, grow, and flourish in ways I never dreamed of when I first heard Shaw's beautiful words.

These are the questions I ask myself, on an ongoing basis:

- What is my purpose in life?
- What is it to be "used by" a "mighty" purpose?
- What is my "mighty purpose?"
- Am I, or am I not, being a "clod of ailments and grievances complaining that the world will not devote itself to making me happy?"

In these final two chapters, let us explore the meaning by examining each of Shaw's phrases.

- What does it mean to "belong to the whole community?"

    - What would my life be like if I felt I had been "thoroughly used up" when I was on my deathbed?

    - Who would I need to be to have my life be "a splendid torch" that I am handing on to future generations?

These are big questions.

As Rainer Maria Rilke says to his protege in *Letters to a Young Poet*:

> *Do not now seek the answers which cannot be given to you because you would not be able to live them. And the point is, to live everything. Live the questions now. Perhaps you will then gradually, without noticing it, live along some distant day into the answer.*

"Live the questions now."

My fervent longing for you is that as you turn the last page of this book and enter the next chapter of your heart-centered life, with an astonishing, extraordinary, and miraculous new opening into joy and service, where your own life is "a splendid torch."

Through the lens of our hearts, then, let's proceed.

"This is the true joy in life."

I hear in this that the "true joy" Shaw refers to arises from within, on its own, when I connect with my authentic self. It does not come from external pleasure or from "getting what I want" or acquiring what society or others think is good for me to pursue, but from listening deeply and sacredly to my soul's true longings and listening deeply for what Spirit is calling me to.

To hear what Spirit is calling for means to listen, deeply, stilling yourself. In the silence, you can hear.

"The Being Used By"

Here, Shaw points to the opportunity to cultivate a profound connection with Source, with the Great Mystery that resides in the invisible realm, beyond all "things" in this world. When we bow, when we let ourselves go, when we surrender to the current, the Tao, to the river of life.

When you are truly "used by," you become fully present. There, in your own wholehearted "Yes" to the universe, you come into joy. You know you are guided from within. You are guided by and connected with Source.

It's not personal; it's more like an energetic force where you are "called," and you answer. You are grateful for the opportunity to be of service to the universe at large. You are a channel.

Each morning, in my morning practice, I ask to be "used by"—I long to be "used by." When I experience "being used by a purpose recognized by myself as a mighty one," I am at peace. I am content. I am home.

"A Purpose"

"What is my purpose in life?" is a question that begs to be asked and re-asked. We looked at this question previously in Chapter 18, and you most likely gave yourself a good entrance into it.

It is truly a lifelong question and requires a commitment to a deep reflection. Inquiring into it necessitates a space of silence and solitude to begin the search.

As Dawna Markova writes in *Wide Open: On Living with Passion and Purpose*:

> *It lives in the rest, in the place where music is born—the fertile void, the silence between notes. It emerges slowly as a sunrise as we search through our gifts, our darkness, our losses and loves. Your job and mine is to be quiet and alone from time. To be present to ourselves and the natural world, and to be in conversation with what is hidden in us to explore what brings us more alive.*

To engage with this question deeply, you may want to spend some time in solitude, venture into nature, or quiet your mind, turning inward until you can hear the voice within you calling you to be. This is a profound and essential quest, as the world constantly tells you who you should be and how you should live. However, the real work lies in discovering who *you* are meant to be.

Who you are meant to be is related to your unique contribution. What is that?

Your unique contribution is not your job.

It is not your resume.

It is not the roles you play—parent, partner, or professional.

It's deeper than that, more essential. It's the thread that runs through everything you do when you are most alive.

It's the stillness that enters your body when you know you are exactly where you are meant to be. It's the love that moves through you when you are giving without needing to be noticed.

Sometimes, I call it your "-ing" verb.

It's not a title, nor an identity. It's a way of being in the world. In a way, it's my mission in life.

So, I love asking the question,

What is the "-ing" verb that I am?

I like "-ing" verbs. They contain an action component, which helps me discern my mission in life.

So the question becomes:

Who am I as an "-ing" verb?

What is the Lifework that I am as an "-ing" verb?

My "-ing" verb is "Awakening."

My friend Ruth's word is "Ministering."

My friend James's is "Touching."

What is the "-ing" verb that you are? Again, trust whatever word or words emerge. Perhaps one will just "pop in." Let it inspire you, even enlighten you.

Or you could start simply inventing words that appeal to you:

- Serving
- Awakening
- Touching
- Enlivening
- Empowering
- Teaching
- Contributing

- Listening
- Exploring
- Evolving
- Caring
- Inviting
- Embracing
- Celebrating
- Appreciating
- Integrating
- Connecting
- Realizing
- Actualizing
- Gracing
- Loving
- Ministering . . .

I wrote the following poem about this:

What is the verb that you are?
I like to ask.
The "-ing" verb:
the word that breathes you,
that sees you,
that be's you,
that speaks you?"
Not the verb that describes what you do—
The verb that says who you are.
The word that breathes you into Being,
and into action.
That unfolds and unfurls and unconceals
Who
You

Are.

What is the verb that you are?

When I landed on the word "Awakening," I knew that was my mission. That word speaks my life.

Thirteenth-century mystic Rumi gets to the essence of the question in his beautiful piece "The One Thing You Must Do."

> *There is one thing in this world which you must never forget to do. If you forget everything else and not this, there's nothing to worry about, but if you remember everything else and forget this, then you will have done nothing in your life.*
>
> *It's as if a king has sent you to some country to do a task, and you perform a hundred other services, but not the one he sent you to do. So human beings come to this world to do particular work. That work is the purpose, and each is specific to the person. If you don't do it, it's as though a priceless Indian sword were used to slice rotten meat. It's a golden bowl being used to cook turnips, when one filling from the bowl could buy a hundred suitable pots. It's like a knife of the finest tempering nailed into a wall to hang things on.*
>
> *You say, 'But look, I'm using the dagger. It's not lying idle.' Do you hear how ludicrous that sounds? For a penny, an iron nail could be bought to serve for that. You say, 'But I spend my energies on lofty enterprises. I study jurisprudence and philosophy and logic and astronomy and medicine and all the rest.' But consider why you do those things. They are all branches of yourself.*
>
> *Remember the deep root of your being, the presence of your lord. Give your life to the one who already owns your breath and your moments. If you don't, you will be exactly like the man who takes a precious dagger and hammers it into his kitchen wall for a peg to hold his dipper gourd.*

*You'll be wasting valuable keenness and foolishly ignoring your dignity
and your purpose.*

–Rumi

Let's dive into the next phrase:

"... recognized by yourself as a mighty one"

I love the three words, "recognized by yourself." This is not your mother's purpose or your father's purpose, or anybody else's purpose, but your own.

What is your *"mighty* purpose?"

You don't have to be Martin Luther King, Jr., or Mahatma Gandhi, or Nelson Mandela, or Rosa Parks—or any of the great leaders and visionaries we know and love who have contributed so much to the world—to be living out of a "mighty purpose."

Yes, all of these leaders, and many more, created stands for their lives out of which they lived. And so can you.

As Matthew Fox says in *The Reinvention of Work: A New Vision of Livelihood for Our Time:*

> *Once one has a spiritual center from which to work, no work (providing it is good work) is alienating; no work is just a job. A person who sweeps floors can, by knowing the meaning of his or her task and appreciating its contribution to the cosmic community's history, sweep floors as an act of sacred work . . . As writer Wendell Berry points out, all work contains drudgery; the issue is whether it holds meaning or not. If we do our work from our center, from our Source, it will always hold meaning.*

My friend Ruth once met a man who introduced himself by stating his name and, in the same breath, said, "I save children's lives."

When Ruth asked him what he did for a living, he replied, "I'm a school bus mechanic."

Allow yourself to let that in.

Similarly, I find the question "What are you building?" to be very powerful.

Even asking the question several times, "And with that, what are you building?" can lead you to a "mighty purpose," one that is much bigger than your small self.

Here is an example:

I get up at 5:30 a.m. for nine months.

With that, what am I building?

The opportunity to let my creative juices flow as I write my book.

With that, what am I building?

The completion of a book that has the capacity to open people to the art of sacred listening; real listening.

With that, what am I building?

People have a new, transformed relationship that works with themselves, others, and life.

With that, what am I building?

The awakening of awareness, heart, spirit, and joy: the awakening of human consciousness.

With that, what am I building?

Inclusion, healing, mindfulness, and right action.

With that, what am I building?

A world that works for everyone, with no one and nothing left out.

And with that, I circle right back to what I stand for.

I first heard that stand—*A world that works for everyone, with no one and nothing left out*—spoken in an evening with Werner Erhard and Buckminster Fuller, who both lived their lives rooted in that stand. When and if (and there have been such moments in my life) I have not lived out of that stand, I have suffered. Since I also stand for joy, I noticed I was suffering and have corrected my own course.

The outer must meet the inner, and if it does not, a tiny part of our spirit dies.

I invite you, whenever you feel moved to do so, to take some time and ask yourself: regarding your life in the world, what are you building? You may want to do that now, or perhaps later, when you give yourself a retreat to delve into this specific work.

Keep going until you are living out of a stand "recognized by yourself as a mighty one."

The next phrase:

". . . the being a force of nature instead of a feverish, selfish little clod of ailments and grievances complaining that the world will not devote itself to making you happy."

I love that phrase. It keeps me grounded. Too often, we unconsciously slip into a mindset of victimhood, as Shaw points out. We see ourselves as victims, while the world—or someone in it—plays the role of the persecutor.

Many of the stories, distinctions, principles, practices, and tools I have shared are intended to support you in disidentifying from the internal voice that keeps you stuck in victimhood and leads to a life of suffering. The opportunity, of course, has been to let go of that voice that is not you, and come into the authentic self that you are, the creator, the artist, of your own life.

Acknowledging Your Accomplishments: Now It's Your Turn

As the artist of your life, let's take a deeper dive below the surface waves; a sacred pause to look at the new canvas of your life now and acknowledge the depth of your work and accomplishments, as well as the new openings you have created through reading the book so far. So, let us take a pause here—a sacred Pause, a Stop—to acknowledge what you *have* accomplished through reading this book.

I have observed that people are sometimes hesitant to acknowledge their accomplishments. Instead of being willing to recognize the ground they have covered, the conversation devolves into some version of "This really isn't important," or "I don't want to brag," or "It probably would have happened anyway."

Please know: acknowledgment has nothing to do with "taking credit." And it has everything to do with completion, with wholeness, with standing for your Self and your good work. Acknowledging accomplishment leaves people with a sense of having made a difference. The "speaking" of it—in this case, the writing of it—requires you to be present in having created something.

I invite you to reflect on where you were when you first began reading this book.

I suspect you bought this book out of a particular attraction, a "longing for" something, or a yearning for something new in your life that you felt was missing. Something drew you to this book. Perhaps it was the word "Sacred," or maybe you knew that listening—real listening—is essential and you don't do that often, or maybe you had a sense that listening could open a new door to creating effective relationships. Or someone told you about it and said it was both entertaining and meaningful. Whatever the reason, something attracted you to this book.

In the introduction, I asked you to address some questions deliberately and intently, and to write in a journal. If you did that, turn to those pages now and see what you wrote. If you did not write, think back to where you were in your life and in your relationships when you started the book. The questions were:

What do you intend to gain by reading this book?

What is a shift, a new opening, or a possibility you would love to create for yourself? What is your heart's deepest desire? What do you long for?

What would you like to move, change, create, or let go of in your life to lead a joyful, meaningful life?

Where are you feeling stuck, held back, or limited in life?

What new possibilities for building relationships—with yourself, with others, and with Life—would you love to explore from here?

If you were to shift from "x" to "y," what would "x" be? What would "y" be?

What specific, personal areas, issues, or concerns would you like to impact in a meaningful, life-giving way? This could be in any domain: professional, personal, work-related, home-related, or community-related.

What are you passionate about that you feel some blockage around? If you experienced a breakthrough in this area, what difference would it make in your life?

Good.

In Chapter Four, *Making This Your Own*, I invited you, once again, to place a relationship in front of you that you wanted to open up, with whom you wanted to create new possibilities.

Please remember what you were thinking, or, if you wrote it down in a journal, read what you wrote.

Good.

Please read each of the following bullets slowly, as a summary of some of the ground we covered. Allow yourself to experience, remember, and reflect upon specific occasions, real moments in time, and real conversations where you made a difference in your life, or the life of another, through:

- Practicing the art of sacred listening; listening to others from your heart to their heart, profoundly and deeply, creating connection, sometimes in the face of disconnection by getting into their world

- Awakening your awareness, intentionally, consciously, and disidentifying from your mind and bringing yourself into full conscious Presence: the Infinite, the Stillness, and the Now.

- Embracing and including, rather than resisting and avoiding, whatever your reactions are to what life is presenting to you.

- Sustaining awareness of your integrity and deepening it, so that inner meets outer as one, and your life is comprised primarily of ease versus struggle—you are living with "no holes in the bottom of your boat."

- Practicing ongoing forgiveness of yourself and others; a practice that offers ongoing access to grace and peace. It enables you to heal yourself and your relationships, restore broken relationships, and free yourself from the baggage of the past. Forgiveness is the key to happiness.
- The practice of stand-taking, and of creating, and bringing gratefulness into your relationship with life; cultivating and building a life worth living, and creating a future from your heart.
- Listening for surprises and recognizing the extraordinary inside the ordinary.
- Creating breakthroughs from breakdowns; seeing the opportunity in breakdowns.
- Allowing yourself to be guided by Source, living and acting in partnership with Source as the place from which to derive what you stand for.

Now, I invite you to stand for what you have accomplished by reading this book. Please take some time addressing whichever of the following questions matter most to you:

What new possibilities have opened up for you in your life through reading this book?

What stories or files have you let go of that opened the door to new possibilities in your life?

Who have you forgiven? What difference has that made?

Where have you created connection in the face of disconnection?

What shift, or transformation, have you made (from "x" to "y")?

Where are you no longer stuck where you were stuck when you started this book?

What new joys are there in your life?

What new possibilities?

Where have you turned a breakdown into a breakthrough?

What new stands have you taken, and in what ways have those stands made a difference in your life?

How has catch, correct, and release made a difference in your life?

What have you accomplished that you might not have accomplished prior to reading this book?

How has deepening your own integrity made a difference in your life?

Where have you been able to meet life with reverence and gratefulness rather than resistance?

How has what you learned changed how you act?

How has your work with this book made a difference in your life or revealed new possibilities?

Once again, I encourage you to pause, recognize, and appreciate yourself for your outstanding work.

Be with this. Be with yourself. Congratulations on your own good work.

We have traveled a long way together in this inner journey.

Now we enter the domain of wholehearted living—a threshold crossing into a way of being that is profoundly awake, connected, alive, and infused with the spirit of Spirit: Service.

> *I slept and dreamed that life was joy. I awakened and saw that life was service. I acted, and behold, service was joy.*
>
> Attributed to Rabindranath Tagore.
> Poet and philosopher

CHAPTER 26

Becoming a Splendid Torch

Living from Service, Joy, and Wholeheartedness

To complete our microscopic deep dive into Shaw's "Splendid Torch" and move to the next part of his declaration, he begins with:

I am of the opinion that my life belongs to the whole community and as long as I live it is my privilege to do for it whatever I can.

That perspective has given me my life for decades.

That view also gave Buckminster Fuller his life. You have probably heard of Bucky Fuller. Bucky was a brilliant man who held twenty-eight US patents, including the geodesic dome. However, his inventions and prototypes are of the least importance to his story, at least to me. I share his story with you here. It is an important story.

Bucky adopted the same viewpoint as Shaw when he was thirty-two. I remember him telling a story at an event I attended with him in San Francisco in the mid-seventies—a story that left a lasting impact on me. In 1927, he was about to become a father with a wife who depended on him financially, yet he was still grieving the loss of his four-year-old daughter from a few years prior. He was broke, unemployed, and saw himself as a "throwaway." Standing on a cliff by Lake Michigan, Bucky was contemplating suicide, ready to jump, thinking he could end his life so his wife could claim his life insurance and start anew.

As he was about to jump, he heard a voice telling him, "You do not have the right to eliminate yourself. You don't belong to you. You belong to the Universe, and your role is to apply yourself to converting your experiences to the highest advantage of others."

This was a profound revelation, one that shifted his perspective on life. Bucky took an oath, "If I never again work for my own advantage and work only for all others . . . I may be justified in not throwing myself away."

He did not jump. Instead, he dedicated himself to what he called "an experiment . . . to find what a single individual could contribute to changing the world and benefitting all humanity."

In other words, "to belong to the whole community and do for it" whatever he could.

Just one person, taking a stand, which required boldness and courage, Bucky published more than thirty books, traveled the world lecturing, and developed numerous inventions, primarily architectural designs.

Faith was Bucky's foundation. He relied totally on the Universe.

In his memoir *Guinea Pig B: The 56-Year Experiment*, Bucky wrote:

> *Friends would say, "You are being treacherous to your wife and child, not going out to earn a living for them. Come over and we will give you a very good job." When persuaded by their obvious generosity and concern, I did yield, everything went wrong; and every time I went 'off the deep end' again, working only for everybody without salary, everything went right again.*
>
> *So, my wife and family have for fifty-six years realized a series of miracles that occur just when I need something, but not until the absolutely last second. If what I think I need does not become available, I recognize that my objective may be invalid or that I am steering a wrong course. It is only through such non-happenings that I seem to be informed of how to correct both my grand strategy and its constituent initiations.*

> *During all these last fifty-six years, I have been unable to budget. I simply have to have faith and just when I need the right-something for the right-reason there it is—or there they are—the workshops, helping hands, materials, ideas, money, and tools.*

That was Bucky's way. It may not be yours, or your friend's, but that was Bucky's way of navigating his passage through life, as he stood for being of service to the planet, trusting that the universe would support him, giving him everything he would need along the way. I, too, stand for a passionate commitment to serving, knowing the Universe supports me. And it always has. (I, however, choose not to live on the brink of bankruptcy!)

But Bucky did. Bucky thrived. He held over twenty-eight patents, funneled $30 million into prototyping the design of his artifacts, published thirty books, and traveled around the world teaching. In an article by Brian Birdwell published on Medium.com, I discovered that although his annual earnings eventually rose to $250,000, he continually reinvested any profit into research and development, "always operating in proximity to bankruptcy without going bankrupt."

Now, that's an example of making a life-altering stand for serving the world, knowing you will be taken care of!

Albert Schweitzer said:

> *I don't know what your destiny will be but one thing I know: the only ones among you who will be truly happy are those who will have sought and found out how to serve.*

Martin Luther King, Jr. put it this way:

> *Everybody can be great, because everybody can serve . . . . You only need a heart full of grace, a soul generated by love.*

Here is where we start.

How do *you* serve?

- Perhaps you serve by listening deeply to your child.
- Perhaps you serve by sharing your wounds with others, as Henri Nouwen suggests.
- Perhaps you serve through your Presence, by being there for another, by looking into their eyes, and by seeing God.
- Perhaps you serve by letting go of your ledger of right and wrong.
- Perhaps you serve by forgiving.
- Perhaps you serve by contributing.
- Perhaps you serve by healing.
- Perhaps you serve by welcoming.
- Perhaps you serve by ministering.
- Perhaps you serve by letting your voice be heard.
- Perhaps you serve by being a school bus mechanic.
- Perhaps you serve by inventing a future to live from (like "a world that works for everyone with no one and nothing left out.")

We've two more lines to explore, the first of which is:

"I want to be thoroughly used up when I die, for the harder I work, the more I live."

What does Shaw mean when he says he wants to be "thoroughly used up?"

Certainly, not that he is spent, abused, harried, or exhausted. Rather, he has been of the highest service possible.

Joy comes from being of service. I think of joyful service as "Wholehearted Living."

In his book, *Crossing the Unknown Sea*, David Whyte, a remarkable poet, describes a time when he felt exhausted because he was no longer engaged in his *true* work in the world. One evening, he had a lengthy conversation with his dear friend, Brother David Steindl-Rast, a Benedictine monk from Austria, whom I have mentioned in this book.

David recounts and pictures the scene for us beautifully:

> *I looked up at Brother David, the nearest thing I had to a truly wise person in my life, and found myself almost blurting, "Brother David?"*
>
> *I uttered it in such an old petitionary Catholic way that I almost thought he was going to say, "Yes, my son?" but he did not; he turned his face toward me, following the spontaneous note of desperate sincerity, and simply waited.*
>
> *"Tell me about exhaustion," I said.*
>
> *He looked at me with an acute, searching, compassionate ferocity for the briefest of moments, as if trying to sum up the entirety of the situation and without missing a beat, as if he had been waiting all along to say a life-changing thing to me. He said, in the form both of a question and an assertion:*
>
> *"You know that the antidote to exhaustion is not necessarily rest?"*
>
> *"The antidote to exhaustion is not necessarily rest," I repeated woodenly, as if I might exhaust myself completely before I reached the end of the sentence. What is it then?"*
>
> *"The antidote to exhaustion is wholeheartedness."*

Let that rest with you for a moment.

That is what I think Shaw meant when he said "thoroughly used up:" living a life of wholeheartedness, full meaning, of dedication, of one-hundred percent-ness. I express it as "no foot out the back door."

Brother David continued:

> *You are only half here, and half here will kill you after a while.*

Often, we are stuck because we haven't fully embraced or created a future worth living.

And so, I ask: What inspired future can you stand for—one that generates an alive, God-filled, enspirited present?

I invite you to engage in this experiment: place yourself at the end of your life and look backwards. Imagine expanding out into the world of infinite possibility, with all your gifts made manifest. What is the life you would love to look back on from your deathbed?

You might want to start with the sentence, "I have lived a life worth living!"

What do you see?

Here are a couple of paragraphs that I wrote when I did this exercise, many years ago:

- I have lived a life worth living!
- We celebrate the awakening of humanity. We have lifted the darkness of the world into the light, the darkness of ourselves into the light. We have transformed our suffering, and that of others, into Love, by Love.
- We live in a world of rich, loving, and connected communication, a world that works for all of us.
- A world in which Spirit is made manifest and palpable through relationship, through integration and integrity, compassion and forgiveness, through connectedness, and through community.
- People are awake to the beauty and extraordinariness around them, to their wholeness and their oneness with all of life.
- We've created a world in which profound wisdom is made available to and through each of us, in partnership with The Mystery.
- Everywhere, people's work is Holy Work: a fulfillment of their gifts, passions, and commitment to making a difference.

Again, I invite you to ask, "What is the life I would love to look back on from my deathbed?"

And, finally, the last of George Bernard Shaw's lines:

"I rejoice in life for its own sake."

Yes!!

"Life is no brief candle to me. It's a splendid torch which I have got hold of, and I want to make it burn as brightly as possible before handing it on to future generations."

Yes, yes, yes!

And how about you? Are you ready to raise that splendid torch high?

Are you ready to have your life *be* that splendid torch?

In fact, I'd like to propose a Yiddish toast as we raise our glowing torches. It was a toast that my father used to love to make, full of the zest for the life that he possessed.

Together, we look each other in the eyes, lift our torches, and say, "L'Chaim!"

"To Life!"

Yes, yes, yes, yes, yes!

Afterword

You are now equipped with new tools and practices for navigating life through open, deep, and sacred listening; I'd like to complete this book as we began, with the blessings I wrote for you at the very beginning.

May *The Heart of Sacred Listening: Transform Your Relationships, Your Work, and Your Life*, be your teacher for a while, your companion, and your guide as the path ahead calls to you to fulfill, as poet Mary Oliver says, your "one wild and precious life."

May you come into the rhythm of the true longings of your heart, finding the extraordinary and the precious within your own core, touching the love and wisdom that lies within, and from which you re-enter into a new world; a world of your own creation.

May others be healed and enlivened by the sacredness of your Presence and your Listening.

May you welcome yourself—your True self—at a new door with joy and elation.

May you find your Self as your own inner teacher, your own Guide.

May you experience all of what life has to offer as a gift.

May you be surprised by who you are and what your life is meant to be at the end of this conversation.

May *The Heart of Sacred Listening* serve as a door to renewal, opening you into your next, New Life.

As you and I part ways now, may you soar out into the world on your own eagle's wings—wings of creativity, joy, laughter, gratefulness, grief, sadness, compassion—the wholeness of life, ready to wholeheartedly lead a **rich**, meaningful existence . . . a life worth living.

With gratitude in my heart, I thank you for the privilege and honor of sharing my journey with you and perhaps guiding you into new territory in your life.

May your ears be fully open to listen. May your eyes be fully open to see.

Tashi Deley

Gratitudes

With deep appreciation, I offer my heartfelt thanks to all who have contributed to the emergence of this book and to the unfolding of my life's work.

Foundational Teachers and Early Guides

I acknowledge my early teachers, mentors, coaches, philosophers, and spiritual guides whose wisdom shaped the terrain on which I walk. Baba Muktananda's unconditional love and spiritual energy—"shakti"—awakened my own and have been sustaining forces throughout my life.

I am profoundly grateful for Werner Erhard's teachings, commitments, and training opportunities, which invited me into a life of possibility, contribution, and service.

I bow to Oscar Ichazo, founder of the Arica School, whose extraordinary weaving of Western psychology, Eastern spiritual traditions, and scientific mysticism formed a deep foundation for my inner development.

The Hoffman Quadrinity Process, a week-long personal growth retreat founded by Bob Hoffman, opened doors for me to complete unfinished parts of the past that were still shaping the present. I am deeply grateful for the stewardship of Raz Ingrasci, whose leadership carried the Hoffman teachings forward and made the work widely available.

I thank Ken Anbender, who trained me as a Communication Course Leader within Werner Erhard and Associates, and with whom I worked for several years at Contegrity, Inc. I am thankful for the growth those years contributed to my development.

I was also privileged to work alongside Gail Cantor, with whom I co-led a program to train Communication Course graduates in enrollment, and whose spirit, partnership, and joy brought both life and depth to our shared work.

I am deeply grateful to Arnold Siegel, whose offering called *The Conversation* guided me with clarity in creating a centered space for myself and Don as we navigated his cancer journey.

Living Teachers Whose Wisdom Continues to Grace My Days
I offer profound thanks to three wise and cherished teachers whose presence and work continue to illuminate my life.

Mark Nepo—whose poetry, books, and in-person circles have blessed my days for many years. *The Book of Awakening*, read almost every morning, has contributed immeasurably to my work with people, as have his other writings. I am indebted to his wisdom, friendship, and extraordinary way with words.

David Whyte—whose poetic brilliance, imagination, extraordinary books, workshops, and Sunday morning sessions continually inspire me, open new territories of reflection and creativity, and offer entrances into deeper layers of being.

Brother David Steindl-Rast—whom I first "met" through David Whyte's *Crossing the Unknown Sea* and later encountered face-to-face when we both participated in Turas d'Anam—has become a dear and blessed friend. His writings, blessings, and the profound teaching of "Gratefulness" have opened countless doors for me and for many others, serving as an essential gateway into Sacred Listening.

Before we parted in Ireland, Brother David offered me a simple instruction: "Stay inspired." Those two words may well have *watered a seed that had long been planted*, serving as an invitation for me to embrace myself more fully as a poet and writer, and to trust what was asking to be written.

With deep gratitude, I honor Lynne Twist, whose inspiring and responsible leadership, life-breathing enthusiasm, unwavering dedication to transforming humanity's relationship with money, and profound commitment to the well-being of both the planet and its people have touched countless lives. Through her example, she has opened doors for so many of us to model what it means to live a committed life and to make a difference wherever we are.

I am especially grateful for her generous offering of the Foreword to this book.

My Irish Family and the Soul of Ireland
A deep bow of gratitude to my adopted Irish family—author, interfaith minister, and singer Nóirín Ní Riain, and her sons, Mícheál Ó Súilleabháin and Owen Ó Súilleabháin—creators and guides of Turas d'Anam. Being in the mystical land of Ireland with them, transported by their harmonized voices, immersed in their poetry, history, and warmth, awakened my own soul and opened a vast space for listening to the Divine.

Those Who Helped Make This Book Possible
The birth of this book has truly "taken a village." My gratitude is immense.

I am grateful for my father, Uma, whose love, vitality, and devotion to my living a full and meaningful life shaped me in ways that continue to resonate through this book. The transformation we shared together lives in my work and in my heart.

I give a deep bow to my husband, Don, whose graciousness, gentleness, and generosity have been a steady presence in my life for over fifty years. His unwavering support has been a source of strength, courage, and grace, and his way of being has shaped the field in which I have been able to breathe, create, and contribute. I am profoundly grateful for his love, partnership, and quiet devotion.

Great thanks to my daughter, Mariel, whose joyful spirit, intelligence, creativity, talent, and humor have graced our lives with joy and laughter.

My gratitude for Ruth Blaney knows no floor. Ruth is a dear friend, an advocate, a companion, a healer, a celebrator of life, a collaborator, a supportive ongoing presence during my medical recovery, and a steadfast partner in bringing transformation to others. To be partnered with her is an honor, a privilege, and a blessing.

I also remember with gratitude Susan London, my first business partner in the early years of my consulting work. Together we created the London/Gale Consulting Group and built a substantial practice with other consultants. It was Susan who introduced the "files" metaphor to describe the stories we carry about one another—an image that has stayed with me. Though our paths later diverged, I appreciate her companionship and what we created together in those formative years.

I acknowledge James Bailey, my coaching companion for thirty years. We have coached one another through countless passages, and I am deeply grateful for his steadfast presence, commitment, and wisdom.

Much gratitude to Marianne Bastin, who partnered with me to make my live courses available while writing this book, and whose deep listening, wise guidance, and unflappable presence supported me through every twist and turn of the journey.

To Bill Weymer, retired CEO of Town & Country Markets, a long-time client whose gentle but persistent "knock on my heart's door," sustained over many years, kept alive the possibility of this book—thank you for never giving up on that vision.

I honor a lineage of leadership stewards whose openness and trust allowed my work to take root and spread throughout the Pacific Northwest. I remember with gratitude Don Nakata, whose wholehearted embrace of the work welcomed me into Washington and into the Town & Country Markets community. His deep enthusiasm and dedication created fertile ground for what followed. Larry Nakata and Bill Weymer carried that tradition forward, generously introducing my work to other leaders and organizations and opening doors to meaningful partnerships with individuals such as Gerry Jones, Tom Brugato, John McGowan, and Kim Hunter of Plymouth Inc., a current client whose loving leadership and deep listening for her people embody this work in the world.

I also acknowledge Jason Parks, whose leadership as CEO of the Pulse Heart Institute initiated The Heart of Leadership within that organization and brought the work into a clinical and institutional context. I am deeply grateful to Dr. Mike Meyers—heart surgeon, former Chief Medical Officer, and now Board Chair—whose leadership revived the initiative and carried it forward during its re-emergence. I also honor Hilary Whittington, current CEO, whose wholehearted embrace of the work has deepened and strengthened its impact.

Together, these relationships, some spanning decades, have shaped not only my work in the world but also the moment when this book was finally ready to be written.

I am deeply grateful for the opportunity to bring Sacred Listening into the business world as a source of workability—what Greg Merten once described as "putting oil into an engine." That doorway opened through Judy McKelvey, who knew me as a Communication Course Leader and introduced me to Gary Egan. Gary welcomed the work into Hewlett-Packard with openness and trust, and through him, Sacred Listening began to find its place in a corporate setting. I also wish to acknowledge Irene Pecenco, who carried that work forward with care and integrity. Greg Merten's partnership, commitment to the work, and the ways he has lived it have been foundational in bringing this work into organizations and allowing it to serve so many.

Diane Merten's own work with forgiveness, born from the loss of her son in an automobile accident, has been a profound contribution to so many. Her willingness to meet that experience with depth and truth has, for over 40 years, opened the space for others to begin to understand what forgiveness truly is. First in *The Heart of Leadership*, and now in this book, her story continues to serve as a doorway for people to discover that possibility within their own lives.

Heartfelt thanks to Susan Allen, whose dear friendship and commitment to "nourishing the quality of life" brought grace and blessing to my days. I also thank Ron Nakata, with whom I partnered for many years to open a new space for the deep development of people within Town & Country Markets. Our partnership lives as joy in my heart.

I extend my deepest gratitude to Leslie McGuirck, a Master Astrologer, intuitive, and psychic, who, during a reading of my natal chart, spoke with unmistakable clarity: "You have to write your book—now. Everything in the Universe is calling for it." She even named a launch window over two years in advance, making the book feel very real long before it existed. That catalytic moment—along with Bill Weymer's steady holding of the book's possibility—propelled me into action.

My gratitude extends to Nancy Hopps, a gifted author and treasured friend, who kindly volunteered as a beta reader. Her page-by-page edits contributed enormously to the book. Her sensitivity to language, her deep understanding of the work, and her generous availability made a profound difference.

To Tommy Dixon, a brilliant writer whose generosity I deeply value, and whose keen instinct for what to include—and what to leave out—enriched the manuscript immeasurably.

To Sandy Robbins, a companion, colleague, and dear friend for many years, for reading substantial portions of the book and offering encouragement at just the right moments.

Heartfelt thanks as well to Joanne Hopkins, my Rolfer and massage therapist, since we moved to the Northwest, whose steady presence has been a source of healing, well-being, and deep clearing for both body and spirit. Her work has been foundational to my life and to my capacity to do the work I love.

Early Readers and "Crossing the Bridge"

I thank my generous first readers, whose early feedback helped shape this book in essential ways. Their enthusiasm gave me great encouragement and meant a great deal, as I had carried a long-standing concern that the written word might not fully convey the transformative power of my in-person work. Hearing from readers who had never worked with me directly dissolved that concern and revealed that the heart of this work does, indeed, make its way across the bridge.

I extend heartfelt thanks to Mike Meyer, Ryan Joy, Ryan Barnes, Dacon Hayes, Tim Tackett, Missy Meyer, Greg Merten, and Diane Merten for reading the book and offering careful and thoughtful feedback.

A deep bow as well to Lloyd Fickett, whose generosity and support urged him to share his wisdom with me in the chapter on moving through Don's cancer—the sharing of which substantially shifted that chapter into one much more grounded, and ultimately deeply satisfying.

A deep bow of gratitude to Hal Isen, whose presence, wisdom, and devotion to awakening have been a quiet and powerful force in my life. His guidance has opened doorways into "I AM," into Being itself, and his partnership has illuminated this work in ways both practical and profound. I am deeply grateful for his freely given support and for the depth of seeing he has offered along the way.

I offer heartfelt gratitude to Jack Canfield for his encouragement, mentoring, and guidance—not only around the book, but around the whole of the work that I am doing in the world.

Creative, Editorial, and Production Partners

I extend warm and heartfelt gratitude to Steve Harrison, whose vision for uplifting authors and amplifying meaningful messages has created a field of support in which this book could grow. Through Bradley Communications, Steve has devoted himself to empowering writers to bring their work into the world with clarity, courage, and reach.

Thank you to Shannon Hazel, my author coach with Team Harrison and Bradley Communications, for her extraordinary expertise, partnership, steadying presence, and cheerleading throughout these nearly two years.

To Valerie Costa, whose editing skills, love for the book, and thoughtful guidance were invaluable. Much gratitude, as well, to Christy Day, whose artistic sensitivity and partnership brought the cover fully alive, reflecting the grace and spaciousness of Sacred Listening.

To the author coaches of Team Harrison—especially Cristina Smith—for their inspiration and centering during this often-rocky journey.

To Mi Ae Lipe, my rigorous and comprehensive guide through the permissions landscape, whose generosity of ideas and care eased the complex process of gathering every necessary permission, and who contributed in so many ways to the book's coming into being.

Special Acknowledgment: Conscious Marketing and Sounds True
I extend a special acknowledgment to Richard Taubinger and Kylie Slavik of Conscious Marketing, whose honest and service-based work in the digital ecosystem has empowered healers, therapists, authors, and coaches to bring their gifts to a wider world. Their integrity, authenticity, and deep commitment to elevating consciousness—while standing firmly in the lineage of wisdom and spirit—have been a profound support to me and to so many of us walking this path.

Richard's visionary leadership helped catalyze and amplify the early online presence of transformative teachers and teachings, including his support of Tami Simon during the formative growth of Sounds True. His capacity to sense what the world is asking for—and to empower those who are bringing it forward—has made a lasting contribution.

Kylie's mastery in storytelling, messaging, and copywriting has opened doors of expression for countless authors, teachers, and creators. Her ability to listen for the deeper current of a story, reveal the heart of a message, and guide others with clarity and generosity has influenced my own creative writing path in enduring ways.

I also honor Tami Simon, whose devotion to making transformative wisdom widely accessible has profoundly enriched my own thinking and that of the global community. Her leadership has cultivated a vast and enduring field of healing and awakening that continues to touch lives around the world.

Leadership, Media, Healing and Wisdom Communities
I am profoundly grateful to those whose platforms, teachings, and institutions have elevated the conversations that matter—through live gatherings, online courses, retreats, and teachings that raise consciousness and support healing across the planet:

Gratefulness.org
The Hoffman Institute
Turas D'Anam

The Esalen Institute
The Kripalu Institute
The Pachamama Alliance
Lynne Twist and The Soul of Money Institute
Stephen Dinan and The Shift Network
Sounds True
Harmony Retreats of Cancer Lifeline

Your dedication to the awakening of consciousness has served countless seekers, including me.

Clients, Retreat Communities, and Leadership Participants

I bow in respect and appreciation to all my clients—past and present—whose courage to transform their personal lives reshapes the cultures they lead and serve.

To my long-term retreat communities, my soul friends, coaching partners, and circles of practice: your mastery, wisdom, love, and hunger for transformation have been enduring sources of partnership in my life and work. I thank you deeply. I am thinking now of DW Green, Rich Duncombe, Susan Allen, James Bailey, Ron Nakata, Larry Nakata, Richard Pedersen, Jan Smith, Joel Larway, Jim Huffman, Bill Weymer, Eric Cress, Evie Merrill, and Marianne Bastin.

Your longing for a workable world—including your own—and your willingness to step forward with courage, joy, and presence have inspired me, again and again.

Closing Gratitude

To all those named here, and to the many unnamed—the visible and the invisible—whose presence, wisdom, love, and quiet acts of grace have touched my life and supported the birth of this book, I offer my deepest gratitude.

May the spirit in which these words were written ripple outward, awakening listening, healing, and open hearts.

Notes

1 **George Bernard Shaw—"A Splendid Torch"**
The two passages presented under A Splendid Torch are drawn from different writings by George Bernard Shaw. They are woven together here to honor Shaw's lifelong conviction that true joy arises from wholehearted service, belonging to the whole community, and living one's life as a gift to future generations.

Permissions & Sources

Grateful acknowledgment is made to the following authors, publishers, and rights holders for permission to reprint or adapt copyrighted material in this book. Every effort has been made to trace and credit original sources accurately. Where appropriate, permissions have been granted and required credit language is included below.

William Stafford

"The Way It Is," from *Ask Me: 100 Essential Poems*. Copyright © 1998 by William Stafford and the Estate of William Stafford. Reprinted with the permission of The Permissions Company, LLC on behalf of Kim Stafford and Graywolf Press, graywolfpress.org.

R. Buckminster Fuller

Excerpt from *Guinea Pig B: The 56 Year Experiment* (1983). Used by permission of the Estate of R. Buckminster Fuller.

Jalāl ad-Dīn Rumi

"The Guest House" and "The One Thing You Must Do," from *The Illuminated Rumi* and *Say I Am You*. Translations by Coleman Barks. Used with permission of Coleman Barks.

David Whyte

Excerpt from *Crossing the Unknown Sea*. © David Whyte. Reprinted with permission from David Whyte and Many Rivers Company, LLC, Langley, Washington, www.davidwhyte.com.

William Stringfellow

Excerpt from *Count It All Joy: Reflections on Faith, Doubt, and Temptation Seen Through the Letter of James*. Used by permission of Wipf and Stock Publishers, www.wipfandstock.com.

Additional Source Acknowledgment
Andrew Auw

"The Gift of Heart Listening," from *Gentle Roads to Survival: Making Self-Healing Choices in Difficult Circumstances*, published by Asian Publishing of Boulder Creek. The publisher could not be located despite reasonable efforts. The author will be pleased to make appropriate arrangements if contacted by the rights holder.

Continue the Journey:
An Invitation Forward

If this book has stirred something in you—a longing to listen more deeply, to live with greater presence, and to bring Sacred Listening more fully into your relationships, your leadership, and your life—you are warmly invited to continue the journey through the following offerings:

Awakening Heart
A Free Substack Offering

If you wish for a gentle companion as you live these practices forward, you are welcome to **Awakening Heart**, Amba's free Substack publication.

Here you'll find stories, poetry, reflections, and teachings devoted to Sacred Listening—and to harvesting life's lessons with grace, humility, and resilience through time.
You can subscribe free here:
https://ambagale.substack.com

The Art and Practice of Sacred Listening
A Leadership Path of Presence, Healing, and Deep Connection
An Evergreen Online Course

An intimate, self-paced online course (just under five hours) offering guided teachings and reflective practices to support you in embodying Sacred Listening in your relationships, your work, and your life.

The Heart of Leadership
A Live, Interactive, Transformational Leadership Experience

A profound, interactive, multi-day leadership immersion inviting break-throughs in leadership of self, others, and life itself. Deep, rigorous, and unexpectedly liberating.

Full descriptions, dates, and enrollment details for both offerings are available at: **galeleadership.com**

About the Author

Amba Gale is a master coach, award-winning author, and lifelong guide for those ready to live and lead with authenticity, courage, and joy. For more than forty years, she has opened new territory in people's lives—empowering them to connect with their own wisdom, beauty, and creativity, and to build relationships rooted in presence, trust, and possibility.

A Phi Beta Kappa graduate of UC Berkeley with honors, and holding a Master's degree in Education, Amba began her career teaching high school English before stepping into the world of transformational leadership. In the 1980s, she founded Gale Leadership Development, bringing her work to leaders, entrepreneurs, and organizations of all sizes. Her approach is not about tips or techniques; it is about creating the listening that transforms individuals, teams, and cultures.

Her award-winning book, *Crossing Thresholds, Island Reflections*, blends poetry, photography, and reflective questions to guide readers through life's passages—from endings to new beginnings. Through her writing, courses, and coaching, she invites people into the practice of Sacred Listening—listening with the whole heart as an act of reverence and connection.

An avid traveler and storyteller, she treasures time with her creative adult daughter and her husband, a musician and songwriter.

Rooted in the natural beauty of Bainbridge Island, Washington, Amba draws daily inspiration from the rippling tides of Puget Sound, the surrounding forest, and the presence of eagles soaring overhead.

www.ingramcontent.com/pod-product-compliance
Lightning Source LLC
Chambersburg PA
CBHW032005050726
47590CB00006B/2048